THE GALLEY SLAVE'S HANDBOOK

THE GALLEY SLAVE'S HANDBOOK

Provisioning and cooking for an ocean crossing

Richard Bevan

THE GALLEY SLAVE'S HANDBOOK
Provisioning and cooking for an ocean crossing

ISBN-13: 978-1453846353
ISBN-10: 1453846352

Sailing; cooking; cruising;
ocean crossing; provisioning

Published by ChangeStart Press, Seattle, WA
info@changestart.com

Available from Amazon.com and other retailers
or order from
https://www.createspace.com/3487131

For George and Peter

Contents

Introduction and acknowledgements

In May and June of 2010 I was a member of the crew of *Neroli of Fowey*, a 1999 Hallberg Rassy 42 owned and captained by Charlie Tongue, for a voyage from St. Lucia to the Azores.

My primary tasks were to be provisioner[1] and cook, and also to write a blog. Allan Collison and Paddy Smyth were the other crew members, and we had invaluable assistance from Charlie's wife, Francoise, during our preparations in St. Lucia.

We had a wonderful experience—challenging, exciting, inspiring, tremendously enjoyable and highly instructive.

Use of the phrase "galley slave" in the title[2] of the book is a shameless attempt to gain attention

---

[1] Or "victualler," as Charlie preferred to refer to my role.

[2] Full credit goes to John Hamwee for this suggestion, along with others that were even more colourful but perhaps not entirely suitable for the family audience. He considered the

and encourage prospective readers to take a look at it. In reality, Charlie was a thoughtful, generous and kindly skipper. Only occasionally—and under extreme provocation from wind, wave, errant crew member or malfunctioning equipment—did the underlying slave-driver personality break through. . . .

It struck me that other victuallers and/or cooks (and even galley slaves) might find some of our experiences and arrangements instructive as a basis for their own planning; and so I've put the material together in this book.

Of course, there are already many treatises that cover the subject in some detail, of which *The Care and Feeding of Sailing Crew*[3] and *The Atlantic Crossing Guide*[4] might be the most comprehensive. And there is a wealth of material available on the Web, Such as the excellent sites www.cruisersforum.com and www.oceannavigator.com.

But perhaps the fresh perspective of a first-timer will be instructive, along with the book's focus on producing good food under challenging conditions. For example, the approach and meals described include (for those so equipped) extensive use of a freezer.

---

originally proposed title ("Recommended provisioning, stowage and cooking arrangements for ocean voyages of short to medium duration by sailing vessel in the Northern Hemisphere") a bit prosaic.

[3] Pardey Books, Arcata, Calif, 1996.

[4] Adlard Coles Nautical, London, 2003.

Needless to say, please use the information with appropriate judgment and scepticism. You'll form your own conclusions about quantities of supplies, meal choices and recipes, storage methods and locations, and other aspects of the plan. You will draw on your own experience and preferences, and those of your crew. But I hope that at least you'll find the book a helpful starting point.

In preparation for the project I compiled a plan that drew on information and ideas from many sources, including guidance from Charlie, his son Henry's work in the same role on *Neroli*'s westbound crossing in 2008, John Payne's *Great Cruising Cookbook*[5] and other references.

The approach also came under Charlie's thorough, pragmatic and constructive scrutiny at frequent intervals throughout the process. Allan and Paddy were tireless food tasters, assistants and advisers in the galley. And the plan was then fully tested, first as we shopped, cooked and stowed in St. Lucia; then as we made our way through the Caribbean and up to Bermuda (an unplanned stop forced on us by equipment issues); and finally on the crossing to the Azores.

Grammar and spelling are for the most part consistent with U.S. usage. So (for example) the onions are yellow rather than brown, we shipped oatmeal rather than porridge oats, and used trash bags instead of bin bags.

---

[5] Sheridan House, Dobbs Ferry, N.Y., 1966.

Recipes mainly use volume measures (cups and spoons) because weighing ingredients on board is usually difficult and sometimes impossible. When weights are needed—to specify meat quantities for example—they are in pounds. Rule of thumb: half a kilo or 500 grams is a generous pound. One ounce is about 30 grams.

Comments and suggestions from readers—whether about meals, quantities, storage, recipes or anything else—will always be very welcome. Please send them to info@changestart.com.

The project

My old friend Charlie Tongue called me on a cold and wet Seattle morning and abruptly said, "What are you going to tell your grandchildren?"

I reminded him that I didn't have any grandchildren. He replied, "Not yet. But you will do one day, and you'll need something to tell them." After a few more exchanges he came to the point: "Will you join my crew to sail the Atlantic next spring? You'll be in charge of provisioning, managing the cooking, and writing a blog."

I've sailed on and off for many years, and sometimes take the family out for a week of chartering in Puget Sound or similar waters. But I'm strictly a weekend sailor. I had never sailed in deep water, or even overnight. So this seemed like quite a stretch.

On the other hand, I know an opportunity when I see one; Charlie is a close friend in whom I have complete confidence; and I love cooking and writing.

As I was gathering my wits and wondering how to respond, my wife, Lesley, walked by. "Charlie wants me to sail the Atlantic with him next spring," I said.

"You have to do it," she said immediately, "as long as you're back for the graduation."

"I'm in," I said to Charlie, "as long as I can get back in time for Nick's high school graduation on 15th June."

"Great!" he said. "The date's no problem. We'll spend the last couple of weeks of April in St. Lucia preparing and provisioning. Then we'll sail up to Antigua, top up our supplies, leave for the Azores in the first week of May and you'll be home by the end of the month."

Of course, that's not exactly how it worked out. We were a little longer in St. Lucia than we planned, had some technical delays as we sailed through the Caribbean (rigging adjustments), and left Antigua a few days later than we'd intended.

Then, a week or so out of Antigua, as we headed north in the trade winds, the generator failed. This was a key piece of equipment: we needed power not just to run the instruments and communication systems, but to drive the water maker, fridge and freezer.

We could have done without all three of these: we had emergency supplies that could have got us to the Azores on pretty basic rations. But we'd have had to run *Neroli*'s main engine to produce power for instruments, lighting and other basic needs (far less efficient at this job than the generator). That would have created a significant risk in reducing fuel supplies in the event of emergency.

So we decided to divert to Bermuda for repairs. These were quickly taken care of, but by then a formidable weather system was approaching whose arrival and passage kept us in dock for another several days.

We finally left Bermuda on May 27. Reaching the Azores in time for me to fly home for my son's graduation still looked feasible, although conditions would need to be good.

As it turned out, the timing couldn't have been tighter. We sailed into Flores (the westernmost island of the Azores) early on the morning of June 13. After various adventures and with the help of a local who befriended us and took it on himself to solve a variety of problems relating to customs, immigration and transport, I made it to an inter-island flight with 20 minutes to spare; made two short hops, and then a third flight to Lisbon; spent the night there; flew to London early on June 14 and picked up a flight to Seattle later that day.

Between Charlie's first phone call and Nick's graduation, I learned a great deal about provisioning for an ocean voyage, about cooking on a 42-foot sailboat, and about much else besides. And while the experience certainly didn't make me an expert, it did teach me many hard-earned lessons that may help other sailors avoid the errors of the first-timer.

So this book combines information from a variety of sources explored in the planning stages with guidance based on the lessons I learned (and the mistakes I made). It includes data about supplies and provisioning (including a full list); recommendations on storage; guidance on cooking at sea and especially in poor conditions; and recipes adapted for shipboard use. The mix is seasoned with some food-related excerpts from *Neroli*'s blog.

The framework

The framework that we used, modified based on our experience, is offered as a starting point for others planning a similar crossing. The underlying premise was that we should have supplies for 28 days[6] (breakfast, lunch, dinner and snacks) with emergency food supplies (storable without refrigeration) for a further 10 days—all for four people.

The emergency supplies were there not in case of an exceptionally slow crossing, but to protect against a catastrophe—for example, a generator failure or other breakdown that could render our frozen and chilled food unusable. *Neroli* was very well equipped with refrigeration. A large fridge and a separate freezer were supported by an effective and economical generator.

---

[6] Our assumption was that this would be more than sufficient for Antigua to Horta—18 to 24 days might be the typical range.

We planned to take 12 complete frozen meals, to be cooked onshore in advance. If that amount of freezer space isn't available to you, then you'll of course need to increase the amount of food taken for preparation at sea. But it's important to note that by leaving out the carbohydrates from most of the precooked meals (potatoes, pasta, rice or other grains were added at sea) we kept the volume pretty small. We were able to pack in all the frozen meals we planned, together with a couple of extras.[7]

In our two weeks of preparation in St. Lucia—with the use of a fully equipped kitchen and a spacious freezer—we cooked triple quantities of each meal. We ate one and froze two more.

Before we met in St. Lucia I had compiled a spreadsheet listing our provisioning needs. This reflected input from many sources, as well as comments and ideas from crew members about their own preferences. We didn't go so far as to identify which meal would be eaten on which day, but we itemized exactly 38 dinners (including the 10 emergency meals) and calculated quantities for the more repetitive breakfasts and lunches.

During this process I began to understand the importance of what perhaps should be the first rule of provisioning: keep it simple. It's far more important that you can quickly and easily find a cer-

---

[7] Along with one or two other small items that came in very useful: For instance, a couple of sheets of puff pastry, some smoked salmon, and extra bacon.

tain item that you have multiple options and alternatives.[8]

For example, most people eat the same breakfast every day. We did not need multiple cereal choices, nor did we need variations on the basic cooked breakfast (appearing a couple of times a week). Availability of leftovers, bread types and choices on how to cook the eggs (for example) create more than enough variation.

Many ocean crossings are made with very basic and simple food, often relying heavily on tinned and dried supplies. For those who are comfortable with that approach, some (or maybe all) of the meals described here may seem too elaborate and complex. But it's also certain that interesting, tasty and nourishing food can be very welcome indeed on a long ocean crossing, and that's what this book aims to encourage.

A cooked breakfast at sea is so welcome that no crew member is likely to grumble that we had the same thing four days before—at least not on a voyage of this duration.

So here is the framework we started with. Once you define your version of this, you can translate the amounts and types of provisions into quantities.

---

[8] Bill Tilman (renowned explorer, mountaineer and sailor; 1898-1977) was said to take a sack each of flour, rice, sugar and oats, and not a great deal else, on his sailing expeditions.

Basic food needs

Breakfast[9]
- For 28 days: tea/coffee, cereal, fruit (fresh or canned), varied bread or toast (made on board), margarine[10].
- For two days each week (8 days in total): the above, plus cooked breakfast of two items from eggs, bacon, sausage, tomato, smoked salmon.

Lunch
- For 28 days: cooked meats (fresh, vacuum-packed, smoked, canned), and/or cheese (fresh and processed), and/or patés (fresh, packet or tinned); bread (made on board); crisp-bread and/or crackers; salad or coleslaw (as long as the ingredients[11] are available).
- For two days each week (8 days in total): the above, plus soup (frozen, packet or tinned).

Dinner
- Two meals precooked (for the first two days at sea)—refrigerated but not frozen.
- Two each of six different meals (12 meals in all) precooked[12] and frozen. Four of these to be fro-

---

[9] See next section for emergency food supplies.

[10] We took only margarine—no butter—based on the crew's preferences and the convenience of the tubs.

[11] We had fresh cabbage all the way—versatile and welcome.

[12] These included a frozen version of each of the refrigerated meals.

zen complete with carbohydrates, for easier preparation in bad weather. For the others, conserve freezer space by cooking the necessary pasta, grains or potatoes at sea.

- Two each of three different "fresh" meals (6 in all) cooked underway. These use mainly fresh ingredients, including long-lasting vegetables, and are accompanied by suitable grains, rice or pasta.
- Two each of four different "packaged" meals, planned for being prepared and cooked underway (8 in all). These used mainly canned or vacuum-packed ingredients (plus grains, rice or pasta).

We added extras (garlic bread, salad, vegetables) depending on what we had available, quantities in the main dish, the crew's appetite and interest, and the cooking conditions.

Desserts[13] approximately twice a week were an extra treat, and backup for days when appetites were not fully satisfied by the main course. Some snacks (see below) also served as desserts or post-dinner or post-lunch extras.

Snacks
To ensure that everyone has snacks that they enjoy, you can invite each crew member to bring a supply

---

[13] The only dessert we needed was canned Ambrosia brand custard with canned fruit—luckily we shipped large quantities of both.

of their own favorites, such as biscuits, potato chips/crisps, nuts, energy bars, chocolate, other candy and dried fruit.

Emergency supplies
These should be packed and stored (if possible) in a separate locker. They can be less accessible than supplies that are expected to be used sooner. Include flour in case conditions permit bread-making.

- Breakfast for 10 days: cereal, milk, crispbread, crackers, rice-cakes, butter and/or margarine[14].
- Lunch for 10 days: canned meat, cheese, crispbread, crackers, rice cakes, butter and/or margarine.
- Dinner for 10 days: canned, dried or otherwise packaged ingredients with pasta, rice or other grains; complete packaged meals—dehydrated or not needing refrigeration
- Water for 10 days. We stored this in the bilges in 2-liter bottles and 5-gallon containers.

In considering emergency supplies, we started with the assumption that the nature of the emergency would probably include a serious accident or problem (loss of power, for example) and not be a simple failure to make the crossing within the 28 days allowed for in the food plan.

---

[14] This will depend on availability of spare refrigerator or freezer space but shouldn't be counted on. By definition, emergency supplies must be able to survive an extended (permanent) power outage.

Accordingly, the emergency provisions had to include water, and had to consist entirely of nonperishable packaged items: dried, canned, bottled or in other long-life packaging.

The one exception to this guideline was margarine, which we included in the emergency list (and stored in the bottom of the refrigerator). We did include oil in the emergency supplies, but we felt that if the emergency included a power failure the margarine would last several days or more, depending on the weather conditions, and could be dispensed with if it became unusable.

From the blog: Profiles and preparations

19 Apr 2010 12:34:00
Rodney Harbour, St. Lucia

On or around May 1, Charlie Tongue, Allan Collison, Paddy Smyth and Richard Bevan will be leaving St. Lucia in the Caribbean to sail to Europe. We will be aboard *Neroli,* a Hallberg Rassy 42 built in Sweden in 1999.

Neroli has a 76-HP Volvo TMD22 engine, a diesel generator, radar and a water maker. Communications equipment includes SSB and VHF radios and an Iridium satellite telephone. Accommodation includes cabins fore and aft, a large saloon with two more berths, galley with gimballed gas cooker, fridge and freezer and two separate heads (bathrooms) with showers.

A four-person team (Charlie, Francoise, Paddy and Richard) are in St. Lucia preparing *Neroli* for the trip. On April 25, Francoise will fly home to England (ash permitting) and the rest of us will leave for Antigua. We'll collect Allan, top up on supplies, and set sail for Europe on or around May 1.

There's quite a bit to be done before the 25th—to put it mildly. More on that in due course. Meanwhile, here's a very brief introduction to the crew.

Charlie Tongue has been sailing for most of his life. In the 10 years that he's owned *Neroli* he's sailed her from Scandinavia to England, Turkey and Croatia; and across the Atlantic in 2008. He's also upgraded, repaired or replaced pretty much every one of the multiple mechanical, electrical and electronic systems aboard to the point where he understands most of them and has personal relationships with suppliers of obscure components on every continent.

He's a thoughtful and meticulous skipper who cares about his crew almost as much as he does about the output temperature of the generator heat-exchanger. He's working very hard (usually below decks in extreme heat and humidity) to get *Neroli* into peak condition for this trip.

Allan Collison is another experienced skipper who has taken his own boat across the Atlantic to the Caribbean (also in 2008) and then back again. The return trip was a solo effort and although it was thoroughly successful he did form the opinion that a variation on a diet of spam and baked beans would be appealing. He's in Antigua for the annual Classics Week and will join the crew when *Neroli* gets to Antigua at the end of this month. Allan brings tremendous sailing experience to our crew and will be able to provide strong support and guidance to the skipper.

Paddy Smyth has a good working knowledge of Nepali and is an expert on altitude sickness, skills that we very much hope won't be called for on this voyage. He's also an anaesthetist (recently retired—he brought the date forward so that he could join this trip) and is *Neroli*'s Chief Medical Officer. Paddy has owned a Halcyon 27 and has many years of experience sailing it around the south coast and English Channel.

In the last few days he's proved to be an extraordinary problem-solver, repairing or upgrading a diverse set of equipment, including the tender's floor, the apartment dishwasher, the emergency grab-bag, the tackle on the lifebelt drogue, the fishing reel and Francoise's broken sandal-strap. Paddy's wife Viv was to join us here to assist in the preparations but sadly was trapped in the UK by the Icelandic volcanic ash.

Richard Bevan joins *Neroli* with somewhat slimmer sailing credentials, although he's sailed irregularly for many years and cautiously skippers family expeditions around the San Juan Islands. A week on *Neroli* in Croatia was not sufficient to deter Charlie from issuing an invitation, although not much to do with sailing appears on the job description. He is in charge of provisioning and with extraordinary support from Francoise has been buying, repackaging, cooking, freezing and generally making a tremendous mess in the kitchen. He enjoys Platinum Elite Frequent Shopper status at the St. Lucia supermarket. He also has the task of maintaining the blog.

Francoise Tongue won't be aboard for the crossing but is very much part of the crew. She has great skills and experience in many aspects of the venture, especially those involving cooking, storage and stowing, making friends with the locals, shopping, negotiating the bus system, dealing with the markets and generally ensuring that we don't take this all too seriously. She is due to fly back to England on 25th April (when everyone else also leaves for England but by a rather slower method) and the question of volcanic ash has been exercising her not a little. But at last count the flights seem likely to be operating again.

Blog entries will be intermittent for the next few days but we will aim to post at least a brief entry on most days once we leave Antigua.

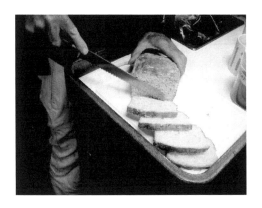

Meal plans

The next step was to translate the overall plan into a listing of specific meals so that we could figure out the quantities we needed. Note that in practice we didn't eat exactly the specified meals in the specified numbers (except of course for the frozen meals— ready to go and always extremely welcome).

Depending on conditions, preferences and availability of supplies—and especially on how well the fresh fruit and vegetables were surviving—the meals were adjusted. For example, we made a couple of homemade soups from leftovers, and a vegetable pie using our carefully preserved puff pastry.

But you could certainly use the meals exactly as specified if you prefer to stick to the plan.

Fresh

We took two meals that we cooked in advance and refrigerated. The idea was to make food preparations especially simple for the first two days as everyone adjusted to life on board—and possibly dealt with sea-sickness.

- Fish pie (1).
- Beef Bourguignon (1).

Frozen

12 meals were cooked and frozen in advance.

- Fish pie—as above (1); carbs are included in the form of mashed potato as the topping.
- Beef Bourguignon—as above (1); carbs (potatoes) were added at sea, although if freezer space permits these could of course be included in the frozen dish.
- Lamb stew (tagine) (2); potatoes added at sea.
- Chicken chilli (posole) (2); carbs (rice or polenta) added at sea.
- Risotto (2); carbs (rice) added at sea.
- Pork casserole (2); potatoes included, but additional carbs (polenta) added at sea.
- Lasagna (2); carbs (pasta) included in the dish as frozen.

Cooked on board—fresh ingredients

6 meals were cooked on board using mainly fresh ingredients.

- Ginger beef St. Lucia (2).
- Special pesto pasta with chicken (2).
- Cabbage, bacon and potato bake (2).

Recipes are included for three other dishes that could be substituted for those above, depending on supplies, energy levels and crew preferences.

- Curried vegetables.

- Fish with Thai curry sauce.
- Steak with vegetables.

Cooked on board— packaged ingredients

8 meals were to be cooked on board using mainly packaged ingredients, but adding fresh as available. In the event, the timing of the crossing meant that we only used two of these.

- Tuna or chicken bake (2).
- Fried rice with ginger and garlic (2).
- Penne carbonara (2).
- Simple pesto pasta with chicken (2)

Emergency supplies

Provisions were carried for 10 meals to be produced using non-perishable ingredients: canned, dried or in a jar.

- Pasta with tomato sauce (2).
- Baked ham with vegetables (2).
- Polenta (2.)
- Curried lentils with rice and naan (2).
- Tuna or chicken bake (2).

The section starting on page 70 includes detailed directions for preparing these meals.

In practice, supplies don't work out exactly. You will find that you run out of some ingredients and have others in excess. In this case you can improvise, adding some leftover chicken to the vegetable curry, or using up some last vegetables in a lunchtime soup, or repeating a dish with some fresh ingredients instead of breaking out the canned supplies.

An important principle on board *Neroli* was that that all major repetitive tasks were shared. Accordingly, all crew members were expected to take their turns in the galley, just as they took their turns on watch. With a range of cooking experience, it was important to plan meals requiring only basic skills. The challenges of cooking in a kitchen that moves in unpredictable and sometimes extreme ways was also something that we had to adapt to.

Our voyage was broken up into two parts by the generator problem, so that after a first leg of only 10 days we were able to reprovision in Bermuda. The next leg took 18 days, so almost all meals had some fresh content; and plenty of supplies were left when we reached the Azores. We even had a couple of frozen meals to be enjoyed after the Atlantic crossing when the crew enjoyed some relaxed cruising around the Azores.

It's worth repeating here the lesson of "keep it simple." When cooking conditions were good (steady sailing on moderate seas, with consistent heel and minimal unpredictable boat movement) it wasn't hard to produce a good meal from the basic ingredients.

But when cooking conditions were difficult (often meaning that sailing conditions were good— downwind perhaps, but with some moderate seas, a great deal of rolling and occasional unexpected wave impacts) it was hard enough to stay secure, let alone to search for obscure ingredients, locate multiple items and cook in more than one pan.

So plan meals that can be cooked in one or at most two pans. Be ready to produce something very basic—if necessary going to the frozen reserves—when conditions in the kitchen make cooking a serious challenge.

But one adapts quickly. Crew members' ability to operate in the kitchen without injury or culinary disaster[15] improved wonderfully as the voyage progressed.

Diet preferences and requirements
Check with all crew members so that you know their likes and dislikes, and also any dietary requirements.

Flexibility on the part of the crew is very helpful. Have that in mind when you are recruiting. Simplicity is a real asset when you are stowing and locating supplies. For example:

- Can all agree on just two or three cereals to keep things simple? (We took Alpen, All-Bran and oatmeal.)
- Can all agree to use margarine (the tubs are easy to store and use) and not to worry about butter?

---

[15] See page 61 for a report on one of the more challenging efforts.

- Can all agree on one grade (e.g., 2% semi-skimmed) of UHT[16] milk?
- Can all agree on caffeinated or decaffeinated coffee—allowing (if decaf) for some caffeinated to be on board for night watches and other times when caffeine might be helpful?
- Can all agree on one kind of tea?

As discussed earlier, suggest that each crew member bring his or her own supply of snacks—chocolate, energy bars, potato chips/crisps, nuts, dried fruit and other favourites. It simplifies planning and ensures that everyone has just what they want.

---

[16] Ultra Heat Treated: Stores for months without refrigeration (but needs refrigeration after opening). This milk is universal in the Caribbean and other warm climate areas and perfect for shipboard use.

From the blog: Progress reports

13 May 2010 22:45:00
28:34.0N 62:24.0W

Technical trouble

A lively night of fast sailing in 20 knots of wind with our "slutter"[17] rig, and a day's run of 121 miles. Around 10:00 a.m. the wind dropped and progress has been much slower. But sailing has taken second place today to a serious equipment problem that's led to a significant change in plans.

Last night the generator failed. It's a key part of *Neroli*'s systems. It runs for several hours each day charging the batteries and providing power for navigation equipment, lights, other systems such as the computer and satellite phone, the fridge and the freezer and—very importantly—the water maker. The main engine can also generate electricity, but it's far less efficient at the job and uses much more fuel to generate the same amount of power; and of course we need to reserve that fuel for emergencies.

It would take too long to discuss the likely cause. Suffice it to say that after working for many hours to identify and address the problem, Charlie determined that it can't be fixed with the resources we have on board.

We then had to decide whether to press on toward the Azores without the generator, or to continue on our present northerly heading to Bermuda, where we could get the issue addressed and then resume the crossing.

---

[17] Sloop-cutter hybrid with a staysail on the inner forestay.

Pressing on was an appealing option in many ways, but would mean the loss of all our refrigerated and frozen food; very strict control of water and other supplies; reliance on our emergency provisions; limited use of instruments; and other limitations. We decided that we have to head for Bermuda. We'll get the generator repaired, top up on supplies and set off again as soon as we possibly can.

We have adjusted to the new reality, will make the most of this brief pause, and of course look forward very much to the second leg of our journey.

27 May 2010 01:45:03
32:32.3N 64:21.9W

At sea again

The generator was quickly fixed, but we have since been pinned down in Bermuda by a major low pressure system with high winds from exactly the wrong direction (east). But the trough has now passed through, the winds have shifted, and although conditions aren't perfect they're certainly good enough. We sailed through the reef this afternoon and are now running downwind steering ENE with the genoa poled out to port.

For the next two days we expect favorable wind conditions, but then there may be a period when we run into headwinds. We continue to talk with Herb Hilgenberg[18]

---

[18] Herb has for many years run a free forecasting service for sailors in the North Atlantic. A legend among those who sail in these waters, he draws on many sources and every day his "clients" call in, report position and

over Single Side Band (SSB) radio and he's helping us pick our way through a fairly complex set of weather systems. We're heading for a waypoint that he suggested, hoping to get no more than one day of northeasterlies before picking up stronger northwesterlies.

Bermuda has dropped below the horizon and once again we're alone on the ocean. Several other boats also left today, headed in the same direction. None are in sight and it's unlikely we'll see any of them again until we reach the Azores.

Our unexpected visit to Bermuda was a delightful break in the journey but we're all very happy indeed to be on the way and settling back into the shipboard routine. After time on shore we need to readapt to the movement—very different from the feel as we sailed up to Bermuda on the wind.

29 May 2010 01:47:00
34:23.9N 62:13.4W

Working our way to the right conditions

We ran 132 miles from noon to noon UTC in a wide variety of wind conditions. Under Herb's guidance we're working our way north, aiming to get to 35N some time tomorrow to pick up winds with at least some component of west in them.

---

intentions, and receive clear guidance on weather systems and wind. We also obtained forecasts via our satellite dial-up, but with slow data transfer these were limited. See http://www3.sympatico.ca/hehilgen.

Early this morning we had 30 knots right behind us and hit 8.5 knots, but our heading wasn't what we needed so the excitement was relatively brief.

For much of the day since then we've been sailing close-hauled with 15 to 20 knots of wind. This is hard work and uncomfortable but it's taking us towards the area where we believe we'll find much more favorable conditions.

Today has been good for wildlife. Our first observation was a large turtle (heading for Bermuda); the second was a group of dolphins that played around *Neroli* for some time.

With wind and wave conditions making cooking a real challenge, this was a good time to go to the freezer. We enjoyed a fish pie (made in St. Lucia) that's already traveled more than 1,500 miles.

A rare sighting was of a Swedish ketch crossing about a mile astern of us. There was no response to our radio call ("Swedish ketch, Swedish ketch, this is Neroli"); we concluded that the vessel was after all a yawl[19], whose crew must have been astonished to learn of the presence of another Swedish vessel—a ketch—nearby.

---

[19] Both the ketch and the yawl have two masts. The mizzen mast of a ketch is forward of the axis of rotation for the rudder: not always easy to discern at a distance.

Guidelines on storage

A theme in these pages is simplicity and consistency. Many deep-water sailors rightly value variation and diversity in their diet. But this comes at the price of complexity in stowage and location of specific items.

That's why our recommendation—at least for relatively short crossings—is to keep it simple. For example, don't take multiple kinds of rice but settle on one or two (Basmati and Arborio would be good choices). Store both in the same area so that when you need it you immediately know where to go.

This will probably be in the same location that you store other packaged carbohydrates: polenta, dried potato, pasta, lentils and couscous. And you (or crew members, perhaps with less cooking experience) have to cook only one or at most two kinds of rice.

It may sound dull, but in bad weather you will value simplicity of access and preparation above all else. And if you are only going to be eating rice four or five times on the crossing—and with different accompaniments—then variation is hardly necessary.

Similarly, standardize on other important bulk items like cereal, oatmeal and flour. Stow them together so that you can quickly locate what you need without having to consult a reference sheet. Designate lockers for rice and other carbohydrates, for breakfast cereal, for flour (we made bread daily), for biscuits and snacks, for canned fruit, for canned vegetables and so on.

We were able to readily agree before the voyage to having just Alpen (muesli), All-Bran or oatmeal for our main breakfast choices. We always had fruit salad as well. This was fresh in the early stages, and later in the voyage it was mostly from cans. Once or twice a week we much enjoyed a cooked breakfast.

But the basic formula was simple. Storing and retrieving the various items was straightforward. When you're experiencing bad conditions and moving around the boat is a challenge—let alone preparing a meal—this simplicity is welcome.

For pre-cooked and frozen meals, it can be helpful to take foil baking trays and form them to fit your freezer space neatly and efficiently. You can freeze meals directly in the trays or place them in plastic bags that can rest in the trays—and take on their shape—while freezing.

Following are storage guidelines drawn from our experience and from that of many others.

Packaging and preparation

- Transfer everything that comes in cardboard[20] packaging into standard, sealed containers that are good fits for your lockers.
- Discard all packaging (along with any resident insects and/or eggs).
- Wash and thoroughly dry fruit and vegetables.
- Particularly wash bananas to keep the fruit flies out. You will have to use bananas fast while in tropical waters.
- Coat eggs lightly in vegetable oil and stow in plastic containers.[21]

Fruit and vegetables

- In the tropics almost everything deteriorates very fast; but once the temperature dropped into the 80s (en route from Bermuda to the Azores) our fresh food lasted much better.
- Not surprisingly, hard fruit and vegetables (potato, onion, apple) store much better than soft ones (eggplant, pear, lettuce).

---

[20] This ensures that all supplies are in standard containers that can easily be stored and stacked, and also that contents stay dry and sealed. It also reduces the possibility that insects and/or eggs join the vessel hidden in packaging.

[21] Some also recommend turning the cartons over every few days; others suggest storing eggs small end down. We didn't do these things but our eggs lasted for four weeks in the bilge—a relatively cool spot.

- Buy some items green and/or hard and bring them out of the fridge gradually: examples of these include avocado, mango and tomato.
- Watermelon survived well at room temperature and made a great basis for fruit salad. Once opened, we stored it in the fridge.
- As fresh fruit was used up we started blending in tins (pears, oranges, peaches, pineapple); we also enjoyed prunes.
- Buy tomatoes green or at least unripe, and store hard avocados.[22]
- These survive well: green apples, citrus, cabbage, potatoes (stored apart from onions), green beans, root vegetables, onions (yellow), garlic, ginger, green tomatoes.
- These survive for a few days (especially if they start unripe): melon, pineapple, mango.
- These do reasonably well but are better kept in the fridge if possible: peppers, carrots, iceberg lettuce.
- Cabbage stores very well, even in the tropics (and cabbage bake—see page 94—can be excellent).
- Don't forget red onions, which can be eaten raw in salads and coleslaw or cooked if other onions are in short supply.

---

[22] Few things are more satisfying than producing a perfectly ripened tomato or avocado a couple of weeks into the voyage. If you have space, store some in the fridge, and bring them out later to accelerate ripening.

- Separate onions[23] from potatoes; yellow or brown onions store better than white ones.

It's worth mentioning here that some dried vegetables can be excellent—especially potato, whether for mash or for hash browns (a great breakfast with eggs).

Storage locations and methods

- Rig nets to store fruit and vegetables: they stay dry and ventilated, and they don't experience impact in rough seas.
- We kept lettuce in the fridge for some time. Iceberg and other dense varieties do best and also provide more weight for a given volume—important in planning fridge space.
- For large items such as melons, lettuce and cabbage we would slice off portions as needed. Once this process started the remaining portion would usually go into the fridge.[24]
- Pineapple doesn't last long while the weather is hot, but if you have fridge space, this can be a great foundation for fruit salad in the early stages of your trip.
- Keep citrus separate (in netting) away from other fruit and vegetables.

---

[23] Onions draw moisture from potatoes and that speeds up deterioration. Onions store best where they can stay dry—they are a good candidate for netting.

[24] Space in the fridge steadily became available as the voyage progressed, of course.

- Keep fruit and vegetables well ventilated—and/or move them occasionally. It's important to check all fruit and vegetables regularly; immediately remove and use (or discard) items that are showing signs of deterioration.
- Root vegetables can be stowed in lockers. Save space (and avoid pests) by removing the tops from beets, carrots and similar vegetables.

From the blog: Competition in the galley

03 Jun 2010 01:58:50
34:47.6N 52:04.7W

120 miles logged, with a bit of a slowdown early this morning when the 15 to 20 knots of wind we'd confidently predicted would take us to the Azores changed its mind and dropped to very little. So we coasted along rather slowly, grumbling about the weather forecasts until dusk when the wind began to pick up again.

Spirits rose with the boat speed. We're now back on track, moving along at about 5 knots, and expecting a gradual increase in wind speed tonight.

The last few days have seen some interesting variations in our diet.

While Richard has overall direction of matters culinary, everyone takes their turn at cooking. Often this involves simply heating up one of our precooked frozen dishes and cooking some suitable accompanying carbohydrate. Tonight, for example, we enjoyed duck confit risotto.

But breakfasts and lunches are open season (subject to availability of ingredients) and Charlie threw down the gauntlet with an extensive cooked breakfast a few days ago.

This featured bacon, although that is in limited supply and in due course we'll move on to ham. Richard followed that with a lunch of croque monsieur. This normally simple dish was quite a challenge: juggling the assembly line on a significantly rolling vessel proved frustrating and—how to put this—a significant proportion of the ingredients escaped.

Allan responded with a dinner dish of fidget pie (slice apples, potatoes, onions and bacon; arrange in deep dish; add stock; bake for an hour; eat with considerable enjoyment). This wasn't on the planned meal schedule but made great use of what was available.

Today Charlie and Richard collaborated on a Salade Niçoise: simple enough, but delightful and surprising in mid-ocean. We have plenty of salad materials although we're conserving them carefully, aiming to extend them for most of the crossing.

You may wonder where Paddy has been in this competitive cook-off. He's collaborated with Allan on a very successful loaf of bread (no insignificant contribution to our comfort and nutrition). But he has also made major innovations on the technology side, as in (for example) his ingenious system for suspending a pan of rising bread dough from hooks in the engine room. And he has, of course, been preoccupied with catching the tuna for the next Niçoise.

By way of warm-up Paddy did secure a flying fish that landed on deck and got trapped in a scupper trying to make its getaway. The cook is still eager to cook flying fish (the national dish of Barbados and a favourite of Sir Francis Chichester on his circumnavigation) but none of sufficient size has yet volunteered.

The provisioning list

The spreadsheet[25] that starts on the next page covers 28 days as described in the overall plan (see page 14) as well as emergency provisions for a further 10. Bear in mind that this list assumes that 12 meals are precooked and frozen or refrigerated.

To the extent that you freeze fewer meals than this—or none at all—then you will need to adjust the quantities and foods in the spreadsheet.

The plan assumes that you will be baking bread. It's a good idea to take a couple of sliced loaves (frozen if possible) so that you don't have to bake for the first few days.

---

[25] If you would like a copy of an Excel file with this data, please send e-mail to info@changestart.com

Supplies are for 28 days plus 10 days emergency but *not including* ingredients for pre-cooked meals (2 refrigerated; 12 frozen). Unless stated, large = 2 lbs; medium = 1 lb; small = 8 ozs.

Group	Item	Notes	Qty	Unit
Carbohy-drate	Biscuits/ cookies	Various	14	pkts
	Cake	Mix	2	pkts
	Cereal	All-Bran	2	pkts (2 lbs)
	Cereal	Alpen or similar	6	pkts (2 lbs)
	Flat-bread	Ryvita and others	12	pkts
	Flour	White	15	lbs
	Flour	Wheat	15	lbs
	Honey	(according to taste/need)	2	jars
	Lentils	Red	2	lbs
	Pasta	Penne/Spaghetti	6	lbs
	Polenta	Cornmeal	2	lbs
	Oatmeal		3	lbs
	Oatmeal	Instant (add hot water)	20	pkts
	Potato	Dried garlic mashed	2	pkts
	Potato	Dried hash browns	2	pkts
	Rice	Various, as preferred	8	lbs
	Sugar: granulated	More if used in drinks	2	lbs
	Sugar: brown	For oatmeal	4	lbs
Dairy—fridge	Cheese	Cheddar and/or Gruyere	2	lbs
	Cheese	Sliced; vacuum-packed	4	lbs
	Cheese	Parmesan: sealable canister	2	lbs
	Cream cheese	Various	2	lbs
	Margarine		10	lbs
Dairy—other	Milk—UHT	Allows one quart per day	30	qts

Group	Item	Notes	Qty	Unit
Drinks	Coffee	Decaf, ground	6	lbs
	Coffee	Regular, ground	2	lbs
	Tea	Regular	300	bags
Emergency[26]	Ham		2	cans
	Cereal		3	pkts (2 lbs)
	Cheese	Grated parmesan	1	jar
	Cookies		5	pkts
	Flour	For one loaf each day	10	lbs
	Jam		1	jar
	Lentils		1	lb
	Marmite[27]	Or Vegemite	1	jar
	Mayonnaise		1	jar
	Milk (UHT)		10	quarts
	Oil—olive		1	pint
	Oil—vegetable		1	pint
	Oatmeal	Quick	12	pkts
	Oatmeal	Regular	1	lb
	Pasta		2	lbs
	Polenta		2	lbs
	Rice		5	lbs
	Ryvita	Or similar flatbread	5	pkts
	Sardines		6	cans

[26] This section of the list is designed to provide food for three meals a day for 10 days. In practice, it's highly likely you will have at least some of the long-lasting fresh food left over—e.g., garlic, onion and other supplies. These will all make the emergency food a good deal more interesting.

[27] For crews from Britain, Australia or New Zealand

Group	Item	Notes	Qty	Unit
	Soy sauce		1	small
	Stock cubes		10	cubes
	Tomatoes		2	tins
	Tuna	Lunch and/or dinner	3	lge cans
	Chicken	Lunch and/or dinner	3	lge cans
	Vegetables	Mixed	2	lge cans
	Water	Large containers	6	5 gal
	Water	Bottled—large	24	quart
	Yeast		12	pkts
	Apples		30	
Fruit and vegetables	Avocado	Firm	12	
	Beets		2	lbs
	Cabbage	White/red/green	4	
	Carrots		6	lbs
	Citrus	Oranges	60	
	Citrus	Lemons, limes	30	
	Cucumber		2	
	Garlic		15	large
	Ginger		1	lb
	Herbs	As available	3	bunches
	Lettuce	Iceberg;; Cos; other dense	6	
	Mango		6	
	Onion	Yellow, medium	24	
	Onion	Red	6	
	Peppers	Assorted colors	6	
	Pineapple		3	
	Potatoes		15	lbs
	Tomatoes		6	lbs
	Watermelon		3	

Group	Item	Notes	Qty	Unit
Household (primary items)	Aluminum foil			
	Cleaning matls			
	Kitchen paper			
	Matches			
	Plastic wrap			
	Tinfoil containers			
	Tissues			
	Trash bags			
	Toilet roll			
	Ziploc bags			
Meat and eggs	Bacon	Sliced	4	lbs
	Bacon	Chopped (lardons)	2	lbs
	Chicken	Breasts/thighs--boneless	4	lbs
	Eggs		6	dozen
	Beef		2	lbs
	Pork chops	Boneless	2	lbs
	Lunch meat		4	lbs
Snacks	Apricots/ mango	Dried	4	lbs
	Candy bars	According to crew taste	60	bars
	Chocolate		12	bars
	Nuts		4	Lge cans
	Potato chips		15	lge pkts
	Prunes		4	pkts or cans
	Raisins		2	lbs
	Various snacks	Supplied by crew members		
Spices/condiments	Baking powder		1	can
	Canola oil		2	large
	Chili powder		1	jar
	Curry paste	Green Thai	1	jar

Group	Item	Notes	Qty	Unit
	Curry powder		1	jar
	Custard	For desserts	8	cans
	Herbs - dried		2	jars
	Ketchup	According to crew taste	2	bottle
	Mayonnaise		2	jars
	Mustard	English	1	jar
	Mustard	Dijon	1	jar
	Olive oil		2	large (quart)
	Paprika		1	jar
	Pesto		4	jars
	Salt/pepper			
	Soy sauce		2	small botts
	Stock	Paste (or equiv in cubes)	4	jars
	Tomato puree	Tubes or small cans	2	cans
	Turmeric		1	jars
	Worcester sauce		1	bott
Spreads	Honey	Plastic, squeezable	2	jars/ pots
	Jam/marmalade		4	pots
	Mango chutney		1	jar
	Marmite		2	medium
	Peanut butter		2	jars
	Other	Based on crew preference		
Cans and jars	Baked beans		4	cans
	Black olives		2	jars
	Chicken		6	large cans
	Chilies		2	cans
	Coconut milk		2	cans
	Ham		4	cans
	Peaches	Unsweetened	4	large cans

Group	Item	Notes	Qty	Unit
	Pears	Unsweetened	4	large cans
	Peas		4	cans
	Peppers	Roasted	2	cans
	Pineapple	Unsweetened	4	large cans
	Salmon	Tinned	8	cans
	Sardines		6	cans
	Soup	Various	12	pkts/cans
	Sweet corn		4	cans
	Thai curry paste	Green	2	jars/cans
	Tinned pate	And similar (for lunches)	4	cans
	Tomatoes		4	large cans
	Tuna		6	large cans
	Yeast	For bread	36	pkts

From the blog: FAQs

11 Jun 2010 21:46:04
38:46.8N 35:12.5W

75 miles in conditions varying from no wind to a good 15 knots. See below ("What do you do if there's no wind?") for a discussion of our present condition. Today's blog tries to answer this and other questions that we think you might be asking.

How much water is *Neroli* carrying?
We have two tanks holding a total of 660 liters—over half a ton. We also carry over 100 liters of fresh water in bottles in case the tanks are compromised in any way by leaks or contamination. With no washing, and using sea water for cooking, that could have lasted us from Bermuda to Horta.

How do you produce additional water?
Neroli's reverse osmosis water-maker can produce up to 60 liters an hour of water, so we have plentiful supplies for cooking, showers and washing. The water costs less than £1 for 100 liters (about 6 cents a gallon). It's purer than rain-water and tastes excellent.

Doesn't this method mean that the water has no electrolytes?
We get all the salts and minerals we need from our rich and varied diet, complete in every respect except for the absence of fresh fish (although we continue to hold out hope that Paddy, whom Charlie has designated Fish Catcher, will come through).

Where is Paddy now?

Paddy is locked in his cabin studying *The Complete Guide to Atlantic Fishing*.

Where does the electricity come from?

A diesel-powered generator produces about one kilowatt, using about a liter an hour of fuel. We run this for a few hours each day to charge the batteries and operate the water-maker. The main engine drives two alternators but uses four times as much fuel as the generator and is only run towards the end of the voyage when there is no wind.

How do you get the blog onto the web?

Neroli is equipped with an Iridium satellite phone. This is an important item of emergency equipment and can also be used to make a dial-up Internet connection. It's slow and expensive, which is why pictures in the blog are few, low-resolution and small. The system is also used for urgent e-mail messages.

What do you cook on?

The stove burns butane. We have five cylinders and just started the fourth.

What do you have for medical emergencies?

We have a comprehensive kit of medical supplies that Paddy assembled.

What's the lighting like?

As well as complete deck and navigation lights, *Neroli* is fully lit below decks with conventional bulbs. She also has red lighting to protect the night vision of the person on watch.

What do you do for exercise?
With the continuing need to shift weight and maintain balance, along with sail-handling and other activity, we seem to burn a surprising number of calories. Despite a hearty diet most crew members have probably lost a few pounds.

We've heard about dolphins, turtles and fish; what about birds?
We're often accompanied by a few seabirds. We believe these are mostly Cory's shearwater; but we have also seen Leach's storm-petrel—especially at night, when their darting, swooping flight makes them appear almost like bats. This morning we saw a group of shearwaters fishing opportunistically when "our" dolphins (regular visitors now by night and day) had evidently driven a school of fish to the surface—or close enough for the shearwaters to dive on them.

How do you navigate?
Neroli carries a very full set of instruments including a chart plotter which is a small computer with electronic charts. We generally work towards a position, called a waypoint, that we put into the plotter, so we can keep a check on our daily progress.

The GPS in the chart plotter provides a very accurate position, and if it were to fail we have a backup.

And of course with Allan and Paddy taking frequent sextant sights, we can always revert to the traditional approach to fixing our position.

How do you steer?

Much of the time *Neroli* is steered by either the Hydrovane, a mechanical self-steering gear that keeps us at a set angle to the wind, or the autopilot, an instrument-based system that can steer relative to the wind or on a fixed course. When conditions call for it we revert to hand steering.

What do you do if there's no wind?

This is a good question for today. With less than 300 miles to go, and the Azores High seemingly entrenched for the summer, we are now motoring. We're watching our fuel consumption and ready to revert to sailing any time we can.

When do you expect to reach the Azores?

Mariners are traditionally reluctant to predict times of landfall—but we're getting closer.

How do you feel about finishing the journey?

We know that we'll be absolutely elated to complete our voyage. We also expect some very mixed feelings about concluding this part of what has been, and continues to be, a wonderful experience.

Cooking at sea

Cooking at sea can be summarized readily: rarely easy, often difficult, frequently frustrating and sometimes dangerous. But it's always an intriguing challenge, and the difficulties are more than compensated for by the satisfaction of producing a good meal under less than ideal conditions.

A task that seems fairly simple and straightforward on land can become a major challenge even in calm seas if the boat is heeling significantly or (worse) rolling on a downwind run.

In the early stages of a voyage some crew members are likely to be a little on the queasy side. We took Stugeron for the first few days. No one was disabled by seasickness but most felt somewhat below par for a while: not badly enough to not want to eat, but certainly enough to reduce the appetite and eliminate any interest in cooking. Going below decks and losing the horizon wasn't appealing.

But as stomachs settled and we adjusted to the movement, cooking became a much more attractive challenge. The frozen meals meant that we always had an easy way of putting a good dinner on the table. We generally reserved them for days when doing more than heating an existing dish and cooking up some rice would have been difficult or dangerous.

For the first two days out we had prepared meals ready to go—not frozen, but complete and needing only heating. The idea was that we would be busy getting everything settled and also might not be feeling 100 percent. Both proved to be the case. Simple meals for this purpose are included in the recipe section of the book.

Breakfast and lunch are just as important as dinner. They maintain energy levels and provide a focal point and break in the shipboard routine.

We settled into a pattern of starting the day with a fruit salad. Initially this was all fresh: mangoes, pineapple, melon, oranges, apple and grapes in the early stages. As the voyage continued and our fresh fruit supplies dwindled, we added tinned fruit to the mix, and also prunes.

This was followed (or accompanied) by cereal or porridge, and then bread or toast. We drank a considerable quantity of tea, but also had coffee at breakfast.

A useful shortcut to a cooked breakfast—even in poor conditions—is to make up an omelette mix in advance: beaten eggs, chopped ham, grated cheese, diced peppers if you have them, perhaps some finely chopped red onion. Save the mixture in Ziploc bags and seal them carefully with the air excluded: then freeze them until needed.

This method can avoid he predicament described in the blog extract that starts on page 61.

Lunch also followed a pattern, alternating among three typical formats. The first (early on, when fridge supplies were good) was cold meat and cheese, with bread and/or crackers, accompanied by a salad. When the lettuce ran out we still had tomatoes, and these, very thinly sliced, with a little red onion, olive oil and lemon juice, were a popular accompaniment to the meats and cheese.

Another standard lunch was chicken, tuna or salmon chopped and mixed with mayonnaise, red onion and any other items that were available— such as red pepper, cucumber or avocado. Sometimes we added a little curry powder to the mix, or perhaps garlic.

And the third standard lunch—for later in the voyage—was a variant of coleslaw, using our long-lasting cabbage, along with whatever hard vegetables were surviving. Carrot was ideal, of course, and we also used onion, garlic, pepper, and apple.

Oven size and efficiency are—on sailing vessels of *Neroli*'s size, at least—quite limited. The recipes in this book are constructed with the recognition that your range of cooking options may be restricted by this, as well as by other challenges of cooking at sea. For example, you may not be able to get more than one cooking pot in the oven—or none at all. All the suggested dishes can be cooked on the top of the stove and with no more than two pans.

Temperature control may not be as good as in your oven at home, and this poses a special challenge when it comes to bread. *Neroli*'s oven may be typical in that the small size means that food in the oven is inevitably close to the flame, so there's a risk of scorching. This was a problem with bread until we devised a heat-shield system in which the baking tin was placed in a larger pan that took the direct heat from the flame.

Bread was a highly important item. We carried 30 or more pounds of flour and baked on most days. In the early stages this was a real challenge, in part because I tried to make it in the same way that I make bread on shore. Dough behaves in unpredictable and sometimes not pleasing ways when challenged by movement, drafts, rapidly changing temperatures and other conditions.

But we settled into a routine—rigorously specified by the skipper in standing orders—using the engine room for rising; fast movement of dough to engine room, and from there to the oven; and the "tin within a tin" heat shield to protect the baking bread from the very close proximity of the oven flame. We had great results.

A bread-making machine would be a great asset. Whatever you think of these devices, they seem to me to be ideal for shipboard use: you don't have to open them, the dough is protected from the various conditions (other than movement) that can lead to collapse or other unsatisfactory outcomes: it remains enclosed, protected and climate-controlled. And cleanup is a great deal easier.

From the blog: Below decks

04 Jun 2010 20:21:00
36:02.0N 50:27.1W

Today's blog will take you behind the glamorous exterior of *Neroli* and her voyage; beyond the glossy facade: relaxing in the sunshine, enjoying tropical drinks, composing Haiku, sampling the cuisine and enjoying peaceful sleep in the luxury guest quarters.

We'll see past the evening studies of the ecliptic under the guidance of Renaissance man Paddy Smyth; we'll look beyond new and ingenious ways of tying two bowlines simultaneously under the keen eye of veteran sea salt Allan Collison; we'll look deeper than practical exercises in shipboard stowing, cleanup and organization led by New Age skipper (or "chief coach" as he likes to style himself) Charlie Tongue.

Let us instead take you into the working portions of the vessel, into the galley for example, where the cook struggles to produce meals worthy of the over-the-top descriptions Charlie used in recruiting Paddy and Allan to this project. To give you some insights into the conditions that we have to work in, allow me to share with you a few highlights from my first shipboard attempt at scrambled eggs.

The conditions were not untypical of this voyage: *Neroli* was close-hauled on port tack. And while that means, in layperson's terms, that the boat is generally tending to lean to the right as you look forward, this isn't guaranteed. Occasionally (quite often, actually, on this particular day) some combination of autopilot, man on watch, wind and/or wave produces a surprising and unheralded move in the other direction.

To add to the fun, encounters with large waves produce an additional kind of unexpected movement in the form of a discontinuous jump that may be (and usually is) in any direction at all, including up and/or down, and if one is holding a container, you and the container may move sharply in the same direction (because one is holding fast to a part of *Neroli*'s interior, as directed by the old maxim, "one hand for yourself, and one for the ship") while the contents of the container (if open) may not feel constrained to move in a similar way and therefore become separated from the aforesaid container, so that if, as is depressingly usual, a further sharp movement in another (e.g., horizontal) direction occurs, then those contents are very unlikely to make it safely back to the container.

(If reading this paragraph has caused you to become short of breath, then perhaps it will give you an insight into the anxiety felt by the ship's cook as he struggled to prepare victuals that met the expectations of the demanding skipper and his ever-hungry crew.)

So there was I, following the "one hand for . . ." maxim, although in my case, and especially when cooking, several more appendages than two hands are called into play.

A hip is wedged into the corner between the stove and the working surface; a knee is braced against the counter opposite; an elbow is wrapped around the post conveniently located nearby, with that hand holding a saucepan; the other hand is clutching the box of eggs in an attempt to keep it under control while breaking the first egg into the bowl in which I am hoping to assemble the eggs prior to scrambling.

The skipper has thoughtfully equipped *Neroli*'s galley with an extensive range of colourful nonslip pads, probably developed by the scientists who brought you sticky-notes.

The idea is that you put one of these on the working surface, then place a container on the pad. The pad won't slide, nor will the container. Unfortunately, as you will very soon learn, other degrees of freedom are usually available.

I managed to break eight eggs into the bowl, and placed it securely (as I thought) on one of the aforesaid nonslip pad. As I attempted to free up a limb to reach past the stove to open a drawer to extract a fork to beat the eggs (and, by the way, another hand is needed here to hold the drawer open while getting out the implement) *Neroli* rolled sharply. (Charlie doesn't like me to use phrases like "lurched wildly" or I would have done so here.)

3M can be proud of the technical achievements of their boffins: the nonslip material performed superbly. Neither mat nor bowl slid. But as the angle increased, most of the contents of the bowl emptied neatly into the sink.

Disaster, you might think . . . but no (not yet) because at least the eggs are still somewhat constrained and perhaps a fast rescue can be effected. But there's not a moment to be lost: the eggs are just about to slide down the centrally placed drain (since for just a moment the vessel is level).

Digression: another blog may have to address this whole thing about working with sinks that are moving oddly and unpredictably and are therefore not amenable to the usual emptying arrangements, not to say pouring scalding water from a kettle that goes off sideways because what your brain says is vertically down into the teacup is actually 35 degrees to the horizontal since the whole galley (kitchen) is leaning and you have no exterior frame of reference (a horizon would be nice but it can't be seen because of the lean; all you see is water racing by just outside the window, looking as if it wants to get in). (End of digression).

But then *Neroli* returned to her previous angle and the eggs slopped to the side of the sink, out of reach of the drain. A mild curse, a couple of dropped implements, a risky move with no hands attached to *Neroli* and I scooped up the eggs (aided by the quality that before I had been aware of but never fully appreciated, that if you can get part of a raw egg under control, the rest tends to follow) and I had let's say 75 percent back in the bowl along with a few coffee grounds and some scraps from Paddy's breakfast bowl (actually, it must have been Allan's bowl because Paddy rarely leaves any scraps).

Luckily three more eggs remained in the box and these were very soon added to the bowl to make up the deficit. Determined to avoid a recurrence, I moved the bowl to starboard (downhill) to the outer edge of the galley (kitchen), next to the locker (cupboard) safely away from the sink (sink) and with the added security of the bulkhead (wall) to wedge the bowl against.

Now I had to light the stove, a process requiring at least three hands: one to hold the lighter; one to turn the knob and hold it pressed in for several seconds; and of course one more to keep me from flying in any one of the several available directions.

As ignition occurred *Neroli* repeated her earlier move, this time with a charming little extra twist that was just sufficient to bounce the bowl away from the bulkhead and enable it to tip again. I watched helplessly, lunging fruitlessly with the gas lighter (though what effect that was supposed to have I can't imagine—perhaps instantly bake the escapees into immobility) as the raw eggs exited the bowl pretty much in their entirety, briefly marshalled themselves, and then began to flow across the working surface towards the albeit distant sink.

For a moment I thought I had a chance to corral them again, using a couple of sponges, a dishcloth and my hands. They had at least half a meter to go across the top of the chest-type fridge. This being a marine-grade piece of equipment, I was confident that it would be equipped with seals around the industrial-weight lid that would keep out the Atlantic, let alone a few wayward uncooked eggs. No such luck.

As the leading edge of the viscous mass reached the lid it hesitated only briefly before taking a sharp downward turn and flowing swiftly and silently into the fridge, the aforementioned property of connectivity of raw egg ensuring that the entire mass, yolk, white and all, took the trip.

I uttered several short words of Anglo-Saxon origin, mostly beginning with earlier letters of the alphabet (credit: Winston Churchill).

I stood silently for a few moments picturing the scene within the carefully stowed fridge and considering what effect eight raw eggs would have as they flowed past the contents and accumulated at the bottom.

I started to raise the lid of the fridge. As I did so I could hear the other crew members, fresh from a relaxing night in their berths, chatting with the skipper in the cockpit as they relaxed over their morning cup of tea.

I let the lid drop and reached for the porridge oats. They need never know.

Landfall

Conditions on the crossing from Bermuda were unusual. At first we encountered headwinds, and later we entered periods of calm as we tried to pick up the southern edge of low-pressure areas or the northern edge of the so-called Azores High. But we worked our way east steadily, if more slowly than we had expected.

Our original destination had been Horta, but we decided to make landfall instead on Flores, the most western of the islands. This would enable me to make flight connections that—if the pieces of the plan fell into place—would get me home in time to attend my son's high school graduation.

The aim was to clear customs and immigration, and get me to the airstrip in time for an interisland flight to Ponta Delgada, where I could connect to Lisbon. The blog relates our arrival in Flores and the subsequent chain of events.

66

From the blog: Landfall at Flores

14 Jun 2010 17:28:02
39:22.7N 31:09.9W

Entry from the skipper

We arrived off Flores in the middle of the night and hove to for a few hours before approaching in daylight. There was some anxiety as to whether this most westerly outpost of the EU would have anyone around first thing on a Sunday morning to clear Richard through customs and allow him to fly out very soon afterwards.

But the guidebook told us that "the friendly Azoreans are renowned for their readiness to help others" and we were not disappointed. Charlie and Richard arrived on the quay at 7:00 a.m. and within minutes were talking with Rogerio, a local fisherman and the only person in sight.

Rogerio was ready to assist. We heard that everything was closed for the weekend, but set off in Rogerio's 20-year-old pickup with Charlie in the cab and Richard[28] standing in the back with the fish boxes. The goal: "find the customs man."

We first went to the custom man's home. There was no sign of him, so then it was off to the custom man's mother's house. She confirmed that he was on holiday.

After a stop at the police station (closed—along with most of Flores, it seemed—after the previous night's disco) Rogerio pondered which of his nine siblings to ask for ad-

---

[28] As I left Neroli in shore-going rig, Paddy commented, "So that's what the well-dressed Seattle pensioner is wearing these days."

vice. Unfortunately, the brother he chose to consult had also been at the disco. Despite loud banging on his front door, he could not be roused.

So then it was back to Rogerio's house to unload the fish and change his clothes. Then we set off again (in another car) to find the police chief in Santa Cruz, 20 kilometers away. All driving was at high speed, with Charlie and Richard's expressions of anxiety greeted by Rogerio with roars of laughter and gratuitous swerves. We took a complex diversion, at Rogerio's insistence, to see calderas, lakes and waterfalls in the island's center.

At last we made it to the Santa Cruz police station. After a lengthy discussion between Richard and the police chief on the quality of Eusebio's performance in the 1966 World Cup semifinal match[29] between Portugal and England, all necessary procedures were completed briskly.

No passports were stamped and no paperwork was issued, but Richard was assured that he could fly out and Charlie that *Neroli* could sail anytime he wished.

After some more sightseeing which included the old harbor and the whaling station, now a museum, we finally made it to the airport. It turned out that the hour and a half we thought we had in hand was actually only half an hour (a slight error in adjusting *Neroli*'s clock on the crossing) —but Richard made his flight and the four subsequent connections that got him home just in time.

The wonderful Rogerio then brought Charlie back to the boat, but only after introducing him to his son Lucas and also to the owner of the petrol station, who agreed to

---

[29] Author's note: I was there. It was a great performance by Eusebio, although England prevailed and went on to win the World Cup.

come to the harbour, collect our four 20-liter fuel cans, refill them and return them to the quay within the hour.

We feel comfortable that customs at Horta will accept our explanation of where the fourth crew member is. They can always ask the Flores police chief—if they can find him.

Using the recipes

The recipes that follow (except for those to be cooked on shore and frozen) are simplified, recognizing that they may be used under challenging conditions. The ingredient lists are short, and omit some components that might be considered nonessential. Of course, you will bring your own recipes and variants (and your own favourite herbs and spices). So if you feel that cinnamon is an essential ingredient in a lamb tagine, by all means add it!

My experience was that looking for a particular herb wasn't always worth the time and effort. The stock included in most of the casserole-type recipes adds flavour and interest, and even if you omit herbs and other flavourings the resulting dish should be tasty. In essence, fry an onion; add some chopped-up meat and brown that; add stock and simmer for a couple of hours and you'll have a pretty good casserole—especially if you can find a bit of garlic and perhaps some wine. . . .

Quantities are mostly stated as volume measures—cups, teaspoons and tablespoons. I use the U.S. size of 8 fluid ounces (16 fluid ounces to the pint) for a cup but in reality it doesn't matter exactly what size you use provided the resulting meal feeds your crew. So I recommend that you test your recipes—we tried them by cooking three of each on shore, eating one for dinner and freezing the others.

One teaspoon is one-sixth of a fluid ounce; a tablespoon is three teaspoons or half a fluid ounce. Again, decide what you will use as a measure and adjust accordingly. Quantities in recipes are very rarely so exact that the difference in size between one teaspoon and another matters. I usually use rounded teaspoons or tablespoons; again, you will determine your own preferences.

For example, if my recipe calls for three or four cloves of garlic, by all means double that (or more) if you have plenty of garlic and everyone likes it; or cut it back (or out) if the reverse is the case. We carried fairly large garlic bulbs—about 50 percent greater diameter than a golf ball—so the cloves were easy to peel and work with.

Many of these recipes call for one medium onion. Again, apply your own judgment and preferences. Our yellow onions survived well (as did the red ones for eating raw with coleslaw and other dishes) so we had plenty available for the entire voyage. We used them generously, particularly in the later stages.

Where volume doesn't work (for example, in specifying quantities of meat or fish) I've used pounds. For those who work and think in metric, a pound is about 450 grams: a little less than half a kilo. An ounce is about 30 grams.

Several recipes call for two pounds of meat or fish (2.2 pounds). For four people this may be a little on the high side unless all have excellent appetites. You can determine exactly what to use based on your crew's preferences or your desire to err on the high side in quantities.

Stock is an important ingredient in many of the recipes. It may not be essential perhaps, but it certainly adds taste and interest. You should be sure to take a generous supply of cubes, powder or concentrate.[30] Remember that stock can be quite high in salt, so don't add any more salt until you've checked the seasoning.

Almost all recipes call for salt and pepper. If possible, freshly ground pepper is best, but of course you will use whatever's available.

Several recipes call for making a gravy or sauce. For those not familiar with the process it's very simple: heat some oil or butter in a pan (say, a tablespoon); add about the same quantity of flour; with the heat low, stir to make a paste (known as a roux) in which all the flour is absorbed and blended with the fat or oil; then before it dries or burns

---

[30] We took several jars of *Better Than Bouillon.* This is available in several versions (including beef, chicken and vegetarian), all of which are excellent.

begin to add liquid—usually stock[31] but by all means include some wine if available. Keep the pan on the heat and stir as you add the liquid. Initially it will become quite thick, but keep adding and stirring until you get the consistency you want.

If you are making béchamel sauce (for Lasagne, for example) the liquid will be milk. It helps the process to have the liquid warm before you begin to add it—especially for Béchamel. If the liquid is cold some of the roux may congeal and then you have to deal with the lumps. A microwave is handy for preheating milk for this purpose although microwaves tend to be unusable at sea because of heel.

Oven temperatures are stated as "very hot" (425°F or 220°C) ("hot" (350°F or 175°C) or "medium" (275°F or 135°C). You probably already know what works best with your oven—or will quickly learn. As always, the more you can test the recipes and your equipment before departure, the better.

We carried olive oil and canola oil (lighter, and cooks at a slightly higher temperature) but used olive oil almost all the time.

The recipes are guides rather than detailed formulas or specific procedures. I'm assuming that at least one person on board (perhaps you) will have some cooking experience, and will be able to adapt the recipes to the situation, conditions and crew's needs and interests.

---

[31] If you make béchamel sauce for lasagne, the roux is butter and flour, and the liquid is milk.

Recipes: for freezing

The recipes in this section are more elaborate than those for cooking at sea, which start on page 92. But all can be simplified. If freezer space is limited you may still decide to use some of those in this section as part of your plan.

If all or most dishes are to be cooked at sea, simplify by sticking to the "core" ingredients (meat and onions, often) and omit extra stages (e.g., preparing bacon bits). At sea you should try to keep the cooking to one or at most two pans.

You can of course use your own favorite recipes. The goal is to keep things as simple as possible for when you're sailing. There are times when cooking— and even elaborate cooking—is possible at sea; but there are many more times when it's a challenge.

All recipes are for four people.

Fish pie

Prepared before departure and frozen.

1 medium onion
1 cup stock
1 cup milk
1-1/2 to 2 lbs of white fish[32]
4 eggs
4 tbsp olive oil
2 tbsp flour
3 lbs potatoes
Salt and pepper

Put the fish in a large pan with the milk, onion and stock. Simmer for about 10 minutes. Take out the fish and cut it into large pieces (2 inches or so), removing any skin. Lay the pieces in an ovenproof dish.

Hard-boil the eggs (6 or 7 minutes). When cool, peel and slice them and spread them over the fish.

Heat half the oil in a pan, add the flour and make a roux (paste); gradually add the reserved cooking liquid, stirring all the time at a gentle simmer to make the sauce.

Season as necessary—with the stock, you may not need any more salt. Pour the sauce over the fish.

---

[32] The cheapest local fish from the Rodney Harbour supermarket worked very well in this pie.

Peel and slice the potatoes and boil for 15-20 minutes until they can just be mashed (don't overcook them). Drain them, mash them and add the rest of the oil (or butter if you prefer, and subject to any dietary limitations of the crew). Season as needed with salt and pepper.

Set the oven to hot (350°F or 175°C). Spread the potato over the fish (adding it in spoonfuls or "blobs" is an easy way of doing it). If you like, sprinkle a little Parmesan or other cheese over the top. Bake for 30 minutes or so until the potato is turning brown.

Beef Bourgignon

Prepared before departure and frozen. If you don't want to add carbs at sea, and have sufficient freezer space, include 2 lbs of potatoes.

2 lbs beef for stewing
2 medium onions, sliced fairly fine
4 or 5 cloves garlic
2 or 3 carrots
2 medium beets
½ cup chopped bacon
½ bottle (or more) red wine
1 tsp mixed dried herbs[33]
2 cups stock
2 tbsp flour
salt and black pepper
3 tbsp olive oil

Put flour in a bowl; season with salt and pepper.
Slice the beef into 1- to 1½-inch pieces; dredge it in
  the seasoned flour.
Sauté the meat in the oil over medium heat, turning
  from time to time, until beginning to brown (4 to 6
  minutes).
Place the meat in a casserole or large saucepan,
  leaving the flour and oil remnants; gradually add
  the wine to those remnants, stirring and scraping
  to make a rich gravy or sauce.

---

[33] If you have separate herbs, sage and thyme work well in
this dish—or use your own preference.

Add the sauce to the meat, then the rest of the wine and the stock. Bring to a slow simmer.

Fry the bacon slowly until crisp and irresistible to passing tasters; add it to the casserole.

Add the onion—with a bit of olive oil if needed—and sauté until soft and beginning to caramelize; add it to the casserole.

Simmer very slowly for at least two hours.

After the first hour or so, add the carrots and beets (sliced or chopped). Add the garlic[34] when there's about half an hour to go. If you want to make the dish complete with carbs, also add the potatoes, peeled and chopped, at the same time.

Check the seasoning and adjust as needed; cook a bit longer if the meat isn't tender.

The phasing of the additions is designed to make sure that while the meat will become tender, the vegetables stay somewhat firm.

The carrots could be cooked and served separately, but for shipboard consumption having everything in the prepared dish makes sense.

Serve with mashed potatoes (if spuds aren't already included); other available vegetables; and a bottle of decent wine if the skipper's attention can be diverted and you can smuggle one aboard.

---

[34] These recipes often call for the garlic being added fairly late in the process. Cooking it less gives an extra flavour and bite to the dish, but if you prefer to add it earlier (and/or fry it first) by all means do so.

Lamb stew (tagine)

Prepared before departure and frozen. Cook this a day ahead of when you plan to freeze it. Then you can skim off any excess fat. But still trim any obvious fat from the lamb.

2 tbsp vegetable oil
2 tbsp flour
2 lbs boneless lamb shoulder, cut into 1- to 2-inch pieces
1 medium onion, chopped
4 cloves garlic, chopped
1 tsp each paprika, cumin and turmeric
1 tbsp (or more, to taste) finely chopped ginger
1 tsp mixed dried herbs (or mixed rosemary and tarragon, if you have them)
Salt and pepper
3 cups stock
1 cup prunes or apricots—no stones
1 or 2 tsp honey, to taste

Mix the flour and spices; season well; toss the lamb pieces in the mixture
In a large casserole, sear the coated lamb pieces quickly in the oil.
Add the onion, garlic, ginger and stock (you can replace some of the stock with wine).
Bring to a slow simmer and keep it there until the lamb is tender—around 2 hours.

(If possible, let stand in the refrigerator overnight and then skim off any fat that's set up on the surface.)

Cut the prunes or apricots into ½-inch pieces and add to the tagine; bring it back to a gentle simmer for 20 or 30 minutes—or a bit longer if you want to thicken the sauce.

Adjust the seasoning if necessary, including adding a teaspoon or two of honey if you wish.

Serve with couscous or polenta, and/or bread.

Chicken chilli (posole)

Prepared before departure and frozen.

2 lbs of chicken thighs (boned and skinless)
2 medium onions
6 cloves garlic
1 tsp dried oregano or mixed herbs)
1 tsp paprika
1/2 tsp chilli powder (less for a mild dish)
Salt and pepper
2 tbsp flour
2 tbsp olive or other oil
1 small can sweet corn (½ cup)
1 small can black beans
1 small jar roasted red pepper (or a fresh one)
3 cups chicken stock
1 avocado (if available), sliced
1 lime (or lemon, if no limes)

Finely chop the onion and sauté until soft; add garlic and continue until onion just begins to brown; add oregano; chop and add red peppers; then set this mixture aside.

Put the flour in a bowl and mix in the paprika and chilli.

Cut chicken into 1½-inch pieces and dredge it in the seasoned flour.

Add more oil to the pan and brown the chicken, turning often (6 to 8 minutes—you may need to do this in two batches, depending on the size of the pan).

Add the onion-garlic-pepper mixture

Add stock (replace some stock with wine if you like); simmer for 10 minutes or so; add black beans and corn; simmer for another 5 minutes or so to thicken the sauce a bit.

Garnish with lime wedges and sliced avocado

Serve with naan or basmati rice (or both).

Risotto

For the garnish (to be prepared before departure and frozen)

1 red pepper (or a small jar)
1 medium onion
3 cloves garlic
Salt and pepper
2 tbsp olive oil
1 medium tin duck confit[35] (2 pieces)

For the rice (to be prepared at sea)
2 cups rice (Arborio if you have it)
2 tbsp oil
4 cups stock, or 3 of stock and 1 of dry white wine
½ cup grated cheese (Parmesan if you have it)

Stage one—on-shore
Open the tin of confit and put the contents (the fat as well as the duck) in a small roasting pan.
Put in a hot oven for 30 to 45 minutes, turning a couple of times.
Pour off the fat and set aside for Other Uses Unlikely to be Approved by Your Cardiologist (e.g., roasting potatoes).

---

[35] If duck confit risotto seems too exotic, you can use the method for a simple vegetable risotto, substituting sautéed or fresh vegetables for the confit. Or you can use chicken, ham or other meat that you have available.

Remove any skin from the duck and break or cut it into small (half-inch) pieces.

While the duck is roasting, chop the onion and pepper; add the oil and sauté the onion until soft (not yet browned); add the pepper and continue to cook the mixture until the onion begins to caramelize; add the garlic for the last couple of minutes.

Remove the mixture from the pan (leave any surplus oil).

Cool and then freeze.

Stage two—off-shore

Thaw out the frozen mixture for an hour or so.

Add 2 tbsp oil to the pan, heat it up a bit and then add the rice, stirring to get it all coated; fry it for a couple of minutes.

Add the wine and let it simmer for a minute or two, then add the rest of the stock; stir it in and then add the garnish (the duck-onion-pepper mixture).

Cover and simmer for 15–20 minutes, checking and stirring occasionally; add a bit more liquid if it seems to be drying out and the rice is still hard.

When much of the liquid is absorbed and the rice is soft and tasty, stir in half the grated cheese (keep the rest for people to add according to individual taste).

If there's no salad or fresh greens, you can add a small tin of peas and/or carrots (or frozen vegetables if you have them) about five minutes before the rice is cooked.

Serve with bread if possible.

Pork casserole with polenta

Prepared before departure and frozen.

1-1/2 lbs trimmed shoulder of pork
½ lb chorizo or spicy sausage
1 chopped red pepper
4 cloves garlic, peeled and chopped
2 medium onions, peeled and chopped
1 tbsp olive oil
1 cup stock
1 cup dry white or red wine (or more stock)
1 large (¾ lb or 400 g) tin tomatoes, chopped
1 tsp mixed dried herbs (or sage and tarragon, if
  available)
2 tbsp flour
½ cup black olives, stoned and halved
Salt and freshly ground pepper
1 lb potatoes[36], peeled and chopped
Polenta or rice (to be added at sea: see separate directions)

Chop the pork and sausage (peeled) into 1-inch
  chunks and coat in seasoned flour.
Add a little oil to a large frying pan and quickly sauté the meat pieces to seal them (not to cook them).
Transfer the meat into a large casserole or saucepan.

---

[36] These are not the main carbohydrate for this dish—that
would be polenta or rice—but a few potatoes add texture and
body to the stew.

Add more oil to the frying pan and sauté the onion
and garlic until it's soft; add the peppers and sauté a minute or two longer. Add all this to the meat.

Add wine and/or stock, tomatoes and olives. Stir
well, put on the lid and bring to a slow boil.

Simmer for about 60 minutes (or place in a medium
oven for the same time).

Add the potatoes and simmer for a further 30
minutes.

Cool and freeze.

At sea, thaw the meal and bring it to a slow simmer.

Serve with polenta (page 121) or rice (page 122).

Lasagne

Prepared before departure and frozen.

This isn't hard to make if you can put together a Bolognese sauce (page 89) and Béchamel sauce (page 91). Once you have those components, making lasagne is simply a matter of assembling the material in layers with pasta. The result is nourishing and satisfying; and since it includes carbohydrates it's an excellent choice for a bad-weather or a day when no one feels much like cooking.

Bolognese sauce (page 89)
Béchamel sauce (page 125)
1 cup grated cheese (mix of Parmesan and another
   cheese—gruyere works well)
1 lb (dry or fresh) or 2 lbs (cooked) lasagne noodles
   or another wide pasta such as penne.

Make the Bolognese sauce using less liquid (just
   one cup of stock) than the recipe on page 89, so
   that the result is fairly thick. Or simmer the mix
   for a bit longer to thicken it.
Prepare the Béchamel sauce.
If the pasta is fresh you can use it directly; if not,
   cook it according to the instructions, though perhaps ending slightly early so that the noodles are
   very much al dente (quite firm).
In a baking dish (or, if you will be freezing this, in a
   tin-foil container) spread half of the Bolognese
   mix.

Add a layer of pasta (use half); if you have lasagne sheets, overlap them.

Pour half of the Béchamel sauce over the pasta.

Add the rest of the Bolognese mix.

Add another layer of pasta.

Add the rest of the béchamel.

Sprinkle grated cheese over the top.

Freeze your lasagne.

To prepare this at sea, let the container thaw: it will take several hours unless you're in the tropics.

Place it in a hot oven for 30 to 40 minutes (or more if you're not sure it was fully thawed).

Bolognese sauce

This recipe is primarily intended for cooking on shore and using in lasagne for freezing, or to make sauce for freezing. But of course it can also be used at sea, probably somewhat simplified. If your supplies are low you can make a good sauce with just an onion, a can of tomatoes, ground beef or sausage, and some seasoning.

2 tbsp olive oil
1 cup bacon or pancetta, diced (will be ½ cup when cooked)
1 medium onion, sliced
½ cup finely chopped carrots
½ cup finely chopped celery
4 cloves garlic, chopped or crushed
Salt and pepper as needed
1 tsp dried herbs (thyme and oregano are good)
1 lb ground beef and/or lamb
1 lb sausage, removed from the casings (if available, use ground pork or more beef; if no sausage available, use extra beef and/or lamb)
1 cup red wine, if available
1 large can tomatoes
2 cups stock (if making this for lasagne, use only 1 cup—the result will be thicker)

In a large frying pan or saucepan, heat the oil over medium heat. Add the bacon and cook, stirring, until it's crisp; set it aside.

Add the onions, carrots and celery (and a bit more oil if necessary); cook, stirring, until soft, 6 to 8 minutes; add this mixture to the bacon.

Add the meat (and a bit more oil if necessary) and cook, stirring, until no longer pink and just beginning to brown (8 to 10 minutes).

Tilt the pan and spoon out the fat that collects: there may be quite a lot.

Add the wine and cook, stirring, to deglaze the pan and remove any browned bits sticking to the bottom, and until about half of the liquid is evaporated (three minutes or so).

Add the tomatoes and their juices, the herbs and the stock.

Bring to a simmer, stirring occasionally to keep the sauce from sticking to the bottom of the pan. After about 60 minutes add the garlic and stir it in well. The sauce should now be thickened and tasty (and the meat tender).

Adjust the seasoning to taste.

If serving over pasta, add the sauce to each bowl separately (rather than mixing it all in) so that if there's too much pasta all the sauce can still be enjoyed. Sprinkle Parmesan or other grated cheese to taste.

Béchamel sauce

This is needed for lasagne. But you can use it in many other ways. For example, toast slices of bread on one side, then place the slices toasted side down on a grill pan. Add ham, pour a little Béchamel over each piece so it's just covered, then sprinkle with grated cheese and grill the result. You now have croque monsieur—an excellent lunch or hearty snack.

1 tbsp butter
1 tbsp flour
2 cups milk (warmed if possible)
Salt and pepper

Melt the butter in a small saucepan.
With the heat low, add the flour and quickly mix it with the butter to form a paste; when all the butter is absorbed add a little of the milk, continuing to stir to keep it smooth.
The mixture will thicken quickly. Keep adding milk, a little at a time, and stirring to keep it smooth. (A whisk can work well at this stage.)
Add seasoning to taste, using white pepper if you don't want to see the particles of black pepper. And some like to add a little nutmeg.
When all the milk is added, keep the heat low and stir until it just begins to simmer. Add seasoning and keep stirring as the sauce thickens. If you want it a little less thick you can add a bit more milk; to thicken it more, keep the heat on (and continue stirring) for a few minutes.

Recipes: fresh ingredients

These recipes will be for cooking in the early stage of the trip while you still have plenty of fresh ingredients—certainly vegetables and perhaps also meat, depending on your preferences and planning.

We took two fresh meals—prepared on shore—in the fridge, for the first couple of days. Those were times when the crew all had a certain amount of initial queasiness, and time below decks (and especially trying to cook) wasn't sought after. But everyone adapted fast and by the third day we were ready to take on more than simply heating a precooked dish.

On other stages of the trip the ginger beef and the pesto chicken were the first two meals cooked aboard. Both are relatively simple, but also appetizing and filling.

Ginger beef St. Lucia

This is based on a dish we enjoyed in a St. Lucia res-taurant. It's a good one to cook the day before depar-ture and hold in the fridge. Then all you need do is heat the dish, and cook some carbohydrates (mashed potato would be good) to go with it.

2 lbs lean and reasonably tender beef[37] sliced into strips (cut off any obvious fat)
½ lb carrots, sliced
1 medium onion, sliced
4 cloves garlic, chopped finely
2 thumb-sized pieces ginger, chopped finely
2 tbsp soy sauce
½ cup red wine
½ cup stock (or 1 cup if no wine available)

Sauté the ginger until it's beginning to brown.
Add the garlic, fry for another minute and then set the mixture aside.
Fry the onions until beginning to brown and add them to the ginger-garlic mixture.
Fry the beef strips for a minute or two on each side to seal and slightly brown them.
Add the soy sauce, wine and stock.
Add the carrots and the ginger-garlic mixture.
Simmer for 10 or 15 minutes.
Serve with pasta, potatoes or rice—or other carbo-hydrate of your choice.

---

[37] We used sirloin steak.

Special pesto pasta with chicken

This[38] is another good dish for preparing before departure: cook the chicken and pesto mixture and keep that in the fridge. Then at sea you only have to cook the pasta and add the pesto-chicken.

1 medium onion
4 cloves garlic
1 lb skinless, boneless chicken pieces OR 1 large or
   2 small tins chicken
1 cup stock
1 jar of pesto (or ½ jar if supplies are limited)
Pasta (see page 119): penne is good in this dish

Chop and sauté the onion.
Add chopped garlic when the onion is nearly done
Set the onion-garlic aside in a bowl.
Slice the chicken into one-inch pieces.
Sauté until lightly browned; check that it's cooked
   through. (If precooked or from a can, sauté just to
   brown it a little.)
Add the onion, garlic and stock.
Cook the pasta and drain it.
Add a jar of pesto and stir in thoroughly.
Add the chicken mixture and serve.

---

[38] It's called "special" to distinguish it from the "simple" version included in the emergency food category.

Cabbage, bacon and potato bake

½ large cabbage or one small one
2 lbs potatoes
2 tbsp olive or vegetable oil
¼ cup finely chopped green pepper (if you have it)
¼ cup finely chopped onion
2 tbsp flour
3 cups stock
Salt and pepper
½ cup grated cheese
1 cup chopped bacon (about ½ cup when cooked)
½ cup bread crumbs

Cut cabbage into chunks (about two inches), removing the hard stalky part.
Peel and slice the potatoes (about ¼ inch thick).
Put potatoes in a large pan and boil for 3 or 4 minutes; add the cabbage and boil for another 2 or 3 minutes (the cabbage should still be slightly crisp and the potatoes firm but beginning to soften).
Drain and place in a baking dish.
While the cabbage and potatoes are cooking, add oil to a frying pan over medium-low heat. Fry bacon bits until crispy; remove and set aside.
In the oil left from the previous step, sauté the pepper and onion until tender and beginning to brown. .
Add flour and stir in to form a paste (roux); gradually add stock, stirring constantly over low heat, un-

til you have a good, smooth (but not too thick) sauce.

Stir in bacon, salt and pepper to taste (won't need much salt, if any).

Pour mixture over cabbage and potato.

Combine shredded cheese and bread crumbs; mix well and spoon topping over cabbage/potato mixture.

Bake in medium oven for 30 to 40 minutes.

Curried vegetables

All the frozen dishes have fish or meat. This dish
   provides a vegetarian contrast.

1 tbsp olive oil
1 onion, chopped
2 medium carrots, chopped
1 cup fresh, frozen or canned vegetables, chopped
1 tbsp finely chopped ginger
6 cloves garlic, crushed or finely chopped
2 tsp curry powder
2 tbsp tomato paste
¼ cup white wine (if available)
1 tsp mixed dried herbs (or just parsley and sage)
1 large (1 lb) tin tomatoes
2 cups stock
½ cup raisins
Salt and pepper to taste

In a large saucepan over medium-high, heat oil and
   sauté the onion, ginger and garlic until soft.
Stir in the curry powder and paste, tomato paste,
   and wine; cook 3 minutes (use stock if no wine).
Stir in the stock and vegetables.
Cook for about 15 minutes or until the vegetables (if
   fresh or frozen) are done; just a few minutes if
   they're all canned.
After 5 minutes, add the raisins
Season with salt and pepper if needed.
Serve with rice (page 122) and naan (page 123).

Fish with Thai curry sauce

This is for when you catch the tuna. On the first day you might want to simply grill some big steaks and enjoy them with potatoes. But on the second day (or perhaps the third if you don't want to dine on fish two nights in a row) this is a great way to do something else with your catch (or to add interest to frozen or tinned tuna or other fish).

The sauce can be made on shore and frozen (doesn't take much space).

1 medium onion, sliced
1 piece ginger (thumb-sized) and 4 cloves garlic, peeled and thinly sliced or chopped
2 tbsp soy sauce
1 tbsp curry or chilli powder
1 tsp honey (or sugar)
1 tsp mixed dried herbs (or parsley, tarragon, and/or sage if you have these)
1 large red pepper, finely sliced (seeds removed)
1 large tomato, diced and with seeds removed39 (or a can of tomatoes)
1 small can coconut milk

---

39 If that sounds too detailed, don't worry about it. But I learned many years ago from Carla Leonardi (proprietor of the Café Lago in Seattle) that if you take out the seeds your tomato sauce (or other dish) will be less acidic and sweeter.

Sauté the onion, ginger, garlic and pepper until soft. Then add the tomato, curry/chili, soy sauce, honey, herbs and coconut milk to the pan and bring to a simmer.

Adjust heat until it is simmering nicely. Cover and cook 6-8 minutes.

Taste for salt and sweetness, adjusting as needed. If too salty or sweet, add lime or lemon juice.

When ready to use the sauce, heat it gently (assuming it was frozen); grill or sauté the fish with a little olive oil and seasoning; pour the sauce over the fish and serve with basmati rice, garnished with lime or lemon wedges.

Steak with vegetables

You could use boneless pork chops instead of steak—depending what's available wherever you are provisioning. This meal requires an extra cooking pot (two usually seem quite enough in a moving galley). One way to deal with this is to cook the potatoes first, mash them and set them aside; then cook the vegetables while you are frying the steak or chops.

4 steaks suitable for frying—e.g., sirloin (8 ounces each)
2 pounds potatoes, peeled and chopped
Fresh vegetables if available; or frozen or canned
Juice of 1 lemon
2 tbsp soy sauce
2 tbsp oil
2 tbsp butter or margarine
Salt and pepper for seasoning

If conditions permit, marinating the steak will improve the result: mix the lemon juice, soy sauce, oil and seasoning and pour it over the steak; leave it for an hour or two.
Place the potatoes in a saucepan of boiling water.
Turn down to a slow boil and cook until you can push a fork through a potato—but stop cooking before they get too soft.
Drain; add butter or margarine, together with seasoning, and mash.
(You can also add a little Parmesan or other grated cheese to add some flavour and interest.)

As soon as the potatoes are done, start the other
vegetables boiling (you can mash the potatoes in a
bowl and re-use the potato water for the vegetables: if they're canned they only need to be heated
and will be ready almost immediately).

Place the steak in a frying pan with the marinade;
fry for a few minutes each side, checking by pierc-
ing with a sharp knife, until done to the taste of
crew members (3 or 4 minutes a side—more if the
steaks are more than about ½ an inch thick).

Drain the vegetables and serve with the steak and
potatoes.

(You could also start the steak when the potatoes
have been on for 10 minutes or so.)

Recipes: mainly packaged ingredients

These are for later in the trip. Also included are suggestions on using leftovers in a soup or pie.

If you have limited fresh food (and freezer space) you may want to adjust some of the earlier recipes to make them compatible with dried and packaged ingredients.

For example, tinned chicken does very well in cooked dishes such as pasta or risotto, where it's mainly adding protein and flavour. The same is true of tuna. When cooking with these, I rinse the meat or fish in cold water after opening the tin—this seems to freshen them up and make them a little more appetizing.

And there is a very wide range of excellent packaged food (freeze-dried, in sealed plastic containers, tins or other packaging). Regular groceries stock these, but you'll find a wide selection in outdoor-activity stores and of course in marine supply stores.

Tuna or chicken bake

In an emergency you can omit all ingredients except the tuna and the pasta, although each of the additional ingredients that you include does improve the dish. Canned chicken can be good, and makes a change from tuna.

2 cups chicken soup made according to the instructions on the packet OR 2 cups stock made with 1 cup of water and 1 of milk
1 large or 2 small tins tuna or chicken, drained and flaked
1 small tin peas
4 cups penne or other pasta (cooked)
1 medium onion, chopped finely
4 cloves garlic, chopped finely
½ cup bread crumbs
½ cup grated cheese

Cook the pasta, drain it and place it in a baking dish.
Use the pan from the pasta to mix the soup.
Add it to the pasta and stir in the tuna, peas, onions and garlic.
Check and adjust seasoning.
Top with bread crumbs mixed with grated cheese
Bake in a hot oven for 20 minutes or until the crust is beginning to brown.

Fried rice with ginger and garlic

To increase protein and interest, add leftover meat, fried bacon bits, or chopped sausage.

4 tbsp oil
2 tbsp garlic, chopped finely (4 to 6 large cloves)
1 tbsp ginger, chopped finely (1 thumb-size piece)[40]
Salt and pepper as needed
½ medium onion, finely chopped
4 cups cooked rice (see page 122)
4 eggs (if available)
2 tbsp soy sauce (can omit if rice is cooked in stock)

Put 1 tbsp of the oil in a large frying pan; turn heat to medium and add the garlic and ginger.
Fry, stirring/turning regularly, until crisp and beginning to brown (3 to 5 minutes).
Take the garlic and ginger out of the pan and put it aside while you cook the rest.
Reduce heat to medium-low; add another tbsp of oil and the onion.
Cook, stirring occasionally, until very soft but not yet brown.
Raise heat to medium and add the cooked rice.

---

[40] This will make a distinctly ginger-flavoured dish—as the name suggests. Halve the amount of ginger for a more subtle result.

Add the remaining 2 tbsp oil; keep stirring and
   scraping it off the bottom of the pan (to avoid
   burning) until it's all hot—this might take 5 or 6
   minutes.
Stir in the soy sauce and garlic-ginger pieces.
Fry eggs in remaining oil ("easy over": white cooked;
   yolk runny).
Serve each portion of rice topped with a fried egg.

Pasta carbonara

You might want to practice this at home or at least on shore (or at anchor): it's a simple dish but judging the amount of water you leave with the pasta is quite important and perhaps worth practicing. I do realize that the direction to "leave about ¼ cup" isn't easy to execute precisely. After seeing the result once or twice you'll be able to make that judgment very well yourself.

Pasta (see page 119): spaghetti or penne is good
2 eggs
½ cup grated Parmesan
1 cup of bacon, chopped into small pieces
Small tin of peas
2 cloves garlic

Fry the bacon until it's crisp.
Add finely chopped garlic a minute or two before the bacon is done.
Drain the fat and set the garlic-bacon mixture aside.
Cook the pasta; drain off most of the water—leave about ¼ cup in the pan with the pasta.
Beat the egg in a bowl with the Parmesan.
Add the egg-cheese mixture and the bacon, garlic and peas (drained) to the pasta.
Stir well over slow heat. In a minute or two the liquid will become creamy as the eggs cook.
Serve with garlic bread (if available).

Simple pesto pasta with chicken

This is a simplified version of the dish on page 94. It assumes limited fresh ingredients.

Pasta (see page 119): penne is good in this dish
I tub, jar or tin of pesto
1 large can of chicken or 2 small ones
Seasoning
Onion and garlic, if available

Chop the onion and garlic finely and sauté until
   soft.
Chop the chicken into one-inch pieces (if it's from a
   tin it will already be in pieces); add it to the on-
   ion/garlic mixture.
Meanwhile, cook and drain the pasta.
Stir in the pesto, along with the chicken.
Serve with grated Parmesan (if available).

Recipes: emergency dishes

Emergency supplies extend the basic 28 days of provisions if necessary. But the main purpose is to provide food if supplies are lost through power failure or another problem. In the North Atlantic, becalming (see image), though frustrating, is unlikely to last long enough to cause a food shortage.

And whatever the cause, there will almost certainly be some usable food from basic supplies. Even if there are just a few items (such as garlic or an onion or two) these will increase the interest and appeal of the meals listed here.

A little creativity toward the end of the voyage can come in useful. Leftover vegetables can be made into a great soup (page 126), or a pie (page 127) if you can come up with some pastry (a couple of sheets don't take up much space in the freezer).

If pastry isn't available, sliced potatoes (partly cooked) make a great topping, as does a mixture of bread crumbs and grated cheese.

Pasta with tomato sauce

1 large can tomatoes
½ cup wine
½ cup stock (or 1 cup if there's no wine to be
  spared)
2 tbsp oil
Salt and pepper to taste
2 tsp dried herbs (one or all of oregano, rosemary,
  sage)
2 tbsp tomato paste
1 medium onion, finely chopped (if available)
4 cloves garlic, crushed (if available)
1 or 2 carrots, finely chopped (if available)

Add the oil to a frying pan, and sauté the carrots
  and onion (if available) until soft (8 to 10 minutes).
Add the tomatoes.
If no fresh vegetables, start by emptying the tomatoes into a suitable pan.
Add the wine or stock, simmer for a minute or two
  and then add the garlic (if available), the herbs,
  and the tomato paste.
Simmer for 15 minutes or so until slightly thickened; adjust seasoning.
Serve with pasta—or any other starch you have left.

Baked ham with vegetables

1 can ham (1½ lbs or 750 grams is a typical size)
Dried mashed potato—amount based on packet size
(most serve four)
1 large can mixed vegetables (e.g., corn, peas and
carrots) or 2 or 3 small cans
Salt and pepper to taste
Margarine or butter (if available)
1 or 2 tbsp grated Parmesan (if available)

The ham can be opened and sliced in advance.
Prepare the potato as directed on the packet: this
will involve adding the contents to a specified
amount of hot water, along with (in most cases)
another packet—included with the dried potato
mix—of seasoning.
Bring a pan of water to the boil and add the drained
vegetables; simmer for one or two minutes to fully
heat; drain and serve.

Polenta as a main dish

3 cups stock (or 2 of stock and 1 cup milk)
Salt and pepper as needed
3 cloves garlic, chopped or crushed (if available)
1 cup yellow cornmeal
2 tbsp olive oil
1 can mixed vegetables (e.g., corn, peas and carrots)
¼ cup grated Parmesan

Add the oil to large pan; sauté the garlic briefly; add
  stock and milk.
Bring to a simmer and gradually add the cornmeal,
  stirring or whisking briskly.
Reduce the heat to low and cook, stirring often, until the mixture thickens and the cornmeal is tender—about 10 minutes.
Turn off the heat. Add the cheese, and stir until
  melted. Add 1 or 2 tbsp of margarine if you have
  any left.
Serve with bread.

Curried lentils with rice and naan

Vegetables if available (onion, garlic, carrot and other survivors)
1 cup uncooked lentils
1 tsp curry powder (more or less to taste)
3 cups stock
Seasoning to taste

Sauté the vegetables until soft and beginning to brown.
Rinse the lentils and drain them.
Stir in the curry powder, add the stock and bring to a slow boil.
Reduce heat and cook slowly (simmer) until done—20 to 30 minutes.
If you have an apple left, peel add it (peeled and chopped) shortly before serving; and/or add ½ cup of raisins.
Serve over basmati rice (see page 122) with naan if available—see page 123.

If you have vegetables available, chop any or all of 1 medium onion, 2 large carrots, 2 stalks of celery and 4 cloves of garlic. Sauté them for a few minutes until soft and add them to the curry, along with a chopped apple and some raisins.

Tuna or chicken bake

This is an "emergency" version of a dish used earlier in the voyage. It omits nonessential (though desirable) ingredients including onion, garlic and cheese. Of course, you should add back any of those you have available.

2 cups chicken soup made according to the instructions on the packet OR 2 cups stock made with 1 cup of water and 1 of milk
1 large or 2 small tins tuna, drained and flaked
1 small tin peas
2 cups penne or leftover pasta (cooked)
½ cup bread crumbs
½ cup grated cheese (if available)

Cook the pasta, drain and place in baking dish.
Use the pan from the pasta to mix the soup. Add it to the pasta and stir in the tuna and peas.
Check and adjust seasoning.
Top with bread crumbs mixed with grated cheese (if available).
Bake in hot oven for 20 minutes or until the crust is beginning to brown.

Bread, pasta, grains and rice

This section contains recipes for various carbohydrate dishes. If you aren't an experienced cook—and therefore are not familiar with managing quantities in the kitchen—you may want to try each of them before the trip and verify or amend the quantities and the process.

Appetites at sea are hard to predict. Depending on the conditions, the crew may be very active for long periods or significantly inactive. Loss of sleep can increase the appetite, and certainly creates opportunities and the desire for snacks. But people react differently to conditions and you need to be ready to adjust quantities as needed.

Availability of good supplies of energy bars, dried fruit, crackers and other snack items is useful not just for midwatch snacks, but also as supplements in case everyone's hunger isn't fully satisfied by one or more meals

Basic bread

2 tsp yeast (or one ¼-oz package)
2 tsp sugar (or honey)
1½ cups warm water
1½ tsp salt
3 cups flour

In a large bowl, dissolve the yeast and sugar in
about 1/2 cup of the warm water.
Stir in the flour and the salt.
Add the remaining water, folding and mixing as you
go. Stop when the dough has pulled together (you
probably will not quite use all the water).
Knead the dough for a few minutes (until "elastic,"
or springy), then put it in a lightly oiled baking
tin.[41]
Place it in a warm place[42] out of drafts.
Cover it with a damp cloth and let it rise until it's at
least doubled in volume (90 minutes to 2 hours).

---

[41] Typically, dough is place placed in a bowl and after rising
initially is "punched down" and placed into a baking tin. For
shipboard purposes it seems sensible to avoid the step of
moving the dough from one container to another.
[42] This isn't always easy to do. If you're in the tropics, finding
a warm place won't be a problem. If not, the engine room can
be a great place to raise dough, assuming that some equipment has been running and that it's warm. If all else fails,
turn the oven on for a couple of minutes and then use that
(remember to turn it off).

Bake in a hot oven for 30-40 minutes or until the
top is golden brown and the bottom of the loaf
sounds hollow when tapped.

*If conditions permit, you can "punch the dough down"
and let it rise a second time before baking; you will
get a slightly more consistent and finer-textured loaf.
But the "once-risen" bread will still be excellent.*

*If you have difficulty getting the dough to rise, you
can mix the yeast and sugar with about ¼ cup of
warm water and leave it for 10 or 15 minutes: it will
become creamy and frothy as fermentation gets started. Then add half of the remaining water and continue with the directions above, next adding the dry ingredients.*

*You can also bake your bread on a baking sheet,
although the dough may spread as it rises, forming
quite a flat-shaped loaf.*

Charlie's foolproof bread

Bread making is something of an art, and the rising of the dough isn't always easy to predict at sea, with movement of the boat, temperature changes and other factors in play.

Charlie's approach[43] takes out the guesswork. If you have any doubt about bread making, you might want to use this approach for at least the first couple of times. The complexity may be worth it to ensure a good result.

Note: This method calls for two people to work together so that one of you has clean hands.

Choose a time when the engine/generator has been running and the engine room is warm.

3 cups flour
2 tbsp butter
1½ tsp salt
1½ tsp yeast (or one packet)
1½ cups warm water

Baking tin
Measuring jug
Large bowl or dish
Damp cloth or tea towel

---

[43] From a recent e-mail from the Skipper: "*The UK Academy of Marine Cookery is pleased to provide the fledgling US school with a bread making recipe that has been proved to work without fail in all conditions regardless of the cook's experience or nationality provided that a timer is used.*"

Fill measuring jug with warm water and put it in
the sink.

Grease baking tin.

Locate a suitable space for raising the dough.[44]

In a large bowl or dish, mix together most of the
flour and all the salt.

Rub in the butter.

Stir in the yeast.

Stir in most of the water.

Knead well for 10 minutes by hand.

Add the surplus flour and/or water as required to
get a firm, consistent but not too wet or sticky
dough.

Shape the dough and place in baking tin.

Place tin in warm place, cover with damp cloth and
leave for 1½ to 2 hours.

Turn on oven to hot.

Remove the cloth and place the baking tin in the
middle of the oven.

Bake for 30-40 minutes or until the top is golden
brown and the bottom of the loaf sounds hollow
when tapped.

Remove loaf from the baking tin and place on rack.

Clean up using seawater (save the fresh) and take
care not to block the sink drain with dough.

---

[44] On *Neroli* we suspended the tin from hooks in the engine
room.

Pasta

Quantities of dried pasta are hard to assess, and so a general rule is to err on the high side (there are many good uses for leftover pasta). One pound of dry pasta is considered generous for four.

1 lb dried pasta
2 tsp salt

In a large pan, bring plenty of water to a boil (as much water as there's comfortably room for, allowing for potential overflow as it boils, movement of the boat and other constraints).

Add the salt and the pasta.

Bring back to a slow boil, using a spoon or fork to make sure that the pasta is not clumping together.

Cook for 5 to 8 minutes, occasionally separating as necessary, until "al dente": there should be some resistance when you bite the pasta, but it should not still be hard. (Cooking time varies according to the type and thickness of pasta.)

Drain and serve immediately.

You may want to add the sauce to individual plates of pasta during serving, rather than mixing it all into the cooking pot. Then, if you have cooked more than enough pasta, each crew member can still get a full share of the sauce and none will be left in the pan with the leftover pasta. Typically, it's not a problem finishing the sauce.

Couscous

2 cups chicken stock
1 cup couscous (about 8 ounces)
¼ cups raisins
¼ cup almonds (can be sliced and toasted – i.e.,
  tossed in a hot pan for a minute)
2 cloves garlic, finely chopped
¼ cup (half a stick) butter, melted

Bring stock to simmer in a heavy, large pot; turn off
  heat.
Mix in couscous, garlic and raisins. Cover and let
  stand until couscous is tender and broth is absorbed, about 15 minutes.
Fluff couscous with fork.
Mix in almonds and butter; season to taste with
  pepper (and salt if necessary).
Transfer to bowl. Serve warm or at room temperature.

Polenta as a side dish

3 cups stock (or 2 of stock and 1 cup milk)
Salt and pepper as needed
3 cloves garlic, chopped or crushed (if available)
1 cup yellow cornmeal
2 tbsp olive oil
¼ cup grated cheese, if available

Add the oil to large pan; sauté the garlic briefly; add
  stock and milk.
Bring to a simmer and gradually add the corn-meal,
  stirring or whisking briskly.
Reduce the heat to low and cook, stirring often, until the mixture thickens and the cornmeal is tender—about 10 minutes.
Turn off the heat. Add the cheese, and stir until
  melted. Add a bit of butter if you like and/or
  cream if you have it, although this seems unlikely
  unless you haven't yet left dock.
Serve with bread and a salad (if available).

Basmati rice

If you miss the soaking phase you might use slightly more water when you cook the rice: 2 cups of water to 1 cup of rice.

1 cup white[45] basmati rice
½ tsp salt (omit if the rice is cooked in stock)
2 cups water for soaking
More water for rinsing
1 ½ cups water or stock for cooking

Wash and rinse the rice.
Add 2 cups of water and leave it soaking for 30 minutes to an hour.
Rinse and drain the rice.
Bring 1 ½ cups of water to boil with the salt OR bring 2 cups of stock to the boil.
Add the presoaked rice; bring back to the boil; turn down heat to simmer; replace the lid.
Simmer for 10 minutes.
When time is up, remove from heat and leave (covered) for another 10 minutes.
Stir the rice and serve.

---

[45] Brown rice will need to be cooked for about 50 percent% longer.

Naan

You may be able to bring naan or similar breads—in sealed airtight packets, frozen or refrigerated. But in calm or reasonably stable conditions it's not hard to make and is a delicious accompaniment to many dishes—especially a curry. This recipe makes eight pieces—plenty for four people if accompanying a main dish as well as rice or some other carbohydrate.

2 cups flour
1 tsp baking powder
¼ cup milk (or ½ cup if yogurt is not available)
¼ cup yogurt, if available
1 tbsp oil
1 beaten egg
½ tsp sugar
½ tsp salt
2 cloves garlic (optional)

Mix the dry ingredients together. Then mix the oil, milk, egg and yogurt and warm it in a pan (or microwave).

If using garlic, crush it or chop it very finely and add it to the mixture.

Gradually add the wet ingredients to the dry ones, mixing until the dough holds together (use a wooden spoon, or at least an implement that won't bend—it's hard work).

There may be a bit of liquid left; add a bit more milk if it's too dry, a bit more flour if it's too wet. Mixture will be tacky but should hold together in one mass.

Let rest, covered, for 45 minutes or an hour.

Lay the dough on a floured surface and cut it into eight pieces, then roll or press them into thin discs.

Heat a very little oil in a heavy pan and fry the naan briefly. It will quickly go brown and bubble a bit. Turn after about a minute or when it looks right.

Other recipes that might be useful

Here you will find a few other recipes that could be useful at some stage of the voyage.

Flying fish may be available simply by picking them up when they land on the deck after hitting the sail or some other part of the boat. Discard the small ones but keep the larger ones. Kill and clean them right away or they'll soon start to go off (assuming the weather is warm).

Coleslaw is a very versatile dish, and a great way of using cabbage in an interesting and tasty fashion. There are endless variations, and when materials for traditional salads (such as lettuce, tomato, cucumber and avocado) run out, cabbage, carrot, apple and other good things will still be available.

125

Leftover soup

A freshly made soup for lunch can be surprising and welcome, especially if there's a new loaf of bread to go with it. And making soup is a practical and useful way of using up scraps of food (especially aging vegetables) that might not be appealing in any other form.

Making soup follows the same principles as many of the other dishes described here: start with slowly fried onion, caramelized for taste and sweetness; add plenty of garlic; add chopped vegetables of any kind, and include meat scraps if available; add a very small amount of flour if you want to absorb excess fat; and then add stock to the roux—a little at first to make something like a rich gravy, and then add more—two or three cups—to make the volume of soup you need. A dash of wine will help, or even sherry or Madeira if you have any on board.

Adjust the seasoning as needed: salt and pepper, of course; a dash of soy sauce, perhaps; or a bit more stock paste or another half-cube if the soup seems bland.

You can serve your soup either as a broth with chunks of vegetable (like minestrone) or apply a hand-held or regular blender if you have one on board to make the soup creamy and consistent in texture.

Leftover pie

Here is the main-meal equivalent of Leftover Soup.

The contents of the pie will of course start with the standard onion and garlic mix, to which you can add the leftovers: probably vegetables, sliced and briefly sautéed. If you don't have many, add some from cans or from frozen supplies.

Add a little stock to provide some liquid, though not so much that the pastry or other crust will be immersed and hard to cook.

Instead of pastry, the pie could be covered with mashed or sliced potato; or breadcrumbs and grated cheese.

Assemble the pie and bake it in a hot oven for about 30 minutes.

Fried flying fish

When eaten with couscous this is the national dish of Barbados. Francis Chichester often ate flying fish[46] for breakfast, and much enjoyed them. If you're busy, in a hurry or working in severe conditions, just season the fillets and fry them.

1 lb (or more) fillets of flying fish
2 cloves garlic, finely chopped or crushed
Juice of a lemon or lime
Salt and pepper to taste
2 beaten eggs
½ cup bread crumbs
2 tbsp oil

Season the fish with garlic, lemon juice, salt and
  pepper.
Dip the fillets in the egg and then coat them with
  breadcrumbs.
Fry in hot oil for 3-5 minutes on each side.
Serve with couscous (or for breakfast with eggs and
  toast).

---

[46] Joshua Slocum enjoyed them also. Some modern mariners assert that flying fish smell bad, but that's probably because they find them on deck in the morning after the fish has been there for several hours in tropical temperatures. If you can get them quite soon after they come aboard they'll be fresh and delicious.

Coleslaw

This useful and simple dish has any number of variations. Listed below are items that you might include—though probably not all at once. Typical basic coleslaw might consist of shredded cabbage, carrot and apple, with a little onion, mayonnaise and salt and pepper. You can mix and match using the list below—or adding other items that might be available.

Cabbage (usually the base—1/2 a medium cabbage will provide a good quantity for four people)
Carrot (1 or 2)
Beet (just a little—it can tend to dominate)
Apple (or pear, if firm)
Red onion (perhaps ½ or ¼)
Mango
Garlic (crushed or chopped very finely)
Raisins
Bacon bits
Mayonnaise and/or lemon juice and/or oil
Salt and pepper
Curry powder

Chop and/or shred and mix your chosen ingredients.
Add a little mayonnaise at a time until you get the texture you want.
A little olive oil can add flavour and keep the coleslaw a little lighter in texture and taste.
Season with your choice of salt, pepper, curry powder, or other items.

Pancakes

4 tbsp plain flour
1 egg, beaten
2 tbsp oil
1 cup milk
½ tsp baking powder
Pinch of salt

Add beaten egg, 1 tbsp oil, baking powder and salt
   to the flour with enough milk to make a paste.
Add the remaining milk and stir well.
Allow to stand for 15 to 20 minutes.
Put the remaining oil in a frying pan; spoon in the
   batter and fry pancakes until golden brown.
Serve with bacon and/or maple syrup and/or eggs.

Oaties

These may be useful if snacks run low. This makes 20-25. For softer and richer oaties, use ½ cup of butter. They may spread to form a single sheet—but you can easily separate them as they cool after baking.

¼ cup butter (or, more likely, margarine)
½ cup sugar
1 egg
½ cup flour
½ tsp baking soda
¼ tsp salt
1 cup oats[47]

Melt the butter.
Mix the dry ingredients, then add them to the butter, mixing well (you'll need a wooden spoon or at least an implement that doesn't bend).
Beat the egg, add it in and continue to mix well.
If you have parchment paper, spread some on a baking tray.
Spoon blobs onto a tray (or form them by hand)—they will be sticky.
Bake in a hot oven for 8 to 10 minutes, or until lightly browned.

---

[47] This would resemble a recipe for Anzac cookies, a national dish of Australia, if it included coconut. But I've omitted that ingredient because I don't like it (gritty) although many people—and most Australians—will want to add it back.

Afterword

From the blog: Reflections from the captain

15 Jun 2010 20:24:49
38:31.8N 28:37.5W

We entered Horta harbour in the Azores at 6:30 this morning and are now berthed in the marina.

It's two months since we arrived in St. Lucia to make the final preparations for the voyage and since then we have sailed over 3,000 miles. During the crossing we seemed to experience more than our share of light or contrary winds. In addition, an unscheduled stop in Bermuda meant that our overall crossing time was extended. But at no time did we experience winds much above 30 knots, at least not when we were at sea. For me personally, the voyage has been an enormous pleasure and a great success. I would therefore like to say thank you:

Firstly to *Neroli* for bringing us safely across an ocean and back into European waters. Although the conditions did not allow her to show her pace, as usual she was at all times comfortable and reassuringly well mannered.

Secondly I would like to thank the crew for making the trip such an enjoyable and memorable experience. Without exception they were magnificent.

Allan's support and advice were truly invaluable. His considerable sailing experience has included two Atlantic crossings, one of which was single-handed, and three visits to the Azores in the last six years. He contributed greatly to the decision-making process on board and enormously increased my level of confidence. He took on the demanding role of Chief Radio Officer, which involved sitting at the radio on most days for two hours at a stretch, listening and talking to Herb, our weather forecaster from Canada. Allan was always upbeat and positive.

Paddy also contributed in multiple ways, very capably filling many roles. As the Ship's Doctor he was an enormous comfort to the rest of the crew even though fortunately his skills were never seriously put to the test. He worked with me to solve the various system and equipment failures we encountered.

As the Astronomer in Residence he ran a nightly seminar on The Sky at Night. Classes were always well attended and brought a wonderful extra dimension to the voyage. He also guided Allan through his studies in astronavigation, and served as Auditor General, monitoring expenditure incurred in four different currencies, by four different people to be shared in four different ways—the spreadsheet was enormous and complex. His contribution was very wide ranging and absolutely invaluable.

And I would like to especially thank Richard, who stepped onto the boat at St. Lucia with relatively little sailing experience and none of it in the dark. It was against this background that he took on the task of provisioning the ship and for providing us with a varied and nutritious diet.

Before we arrived in St. Lucia he prepared a list of the supplies that the four of us would need. He then took responsibility for all the shopping, the cooking and freezing of a dozen meals; and finally for the stowage on board.

As soon as we set off, he took control of the galley and supplied us (with some help from the rest of the crew) with one wonderful meal after another. If that was not enough, he also took responsibility for our daily Web Diary.

No matter what the weather was like, no matter how tired he was, a blog was posted every day. For a period of six weeks, he gave considerable pleasure to a large number of the crew's friends and family ashore. On behalf of blog readers everywhere, a very big thank you!

I would also like to thank our four wives, Diana, Viv, Lesley and Francoise, for encouraging four old men to go out and make believe that they were young again! My special thanks to Francoise for all her support in St. Lucia, where she worked long hours for ten days with Richard, shopping, cooking food for freezing, and assisting in packaging and stowage.

Finally thanks to all our readers for sharing this voyage with us. I very much hope you have enjoyed the experience.

To have the opportunity to sail across an ocean in a small boat is definitely a privilege. As the days pass, the emptiness, the isolation and the wild beauty of the surroundings touch the senses and then at night, sooner or later, Creation puts on one of its most spectacular shows— a moonlit sea and a clear sky filled with a million stars, stretching without interruption from horizon to horizon in every direction, as far as the eye can see.

This private viewing is most certainly a privilege. It tells us emphatically that we live in a universe of infinite scale, incomprehensible permanence and wondrous predictability.

Charlie Tongue
Neroli
15th June 2010

3954238R00077

Printed in Great Britain
by Amazon.co.uk, Ltd.,
Marston Gate.